Houghton
Mifflin
Harcourt

# MATH Expressions
## Common Core

Dr. Karen C. Fuson

GRADE

**3**

Volume 1

This material is based upon work supported by the
**National Science Foundation**
under Grant Numbers
ESI-9816320, REC-9806020, and RED-935373.

Any opinions, findings, and conclusions, or recommendations expressed in this material
are those of the author and do not necessarily reflect the views of the National Science Foundation.

# VOLUME 1 CONTENTS

## UNIT 1 Multiplication and Division with 0–5, 9 and 10

© Houghton Mifflin Harcourt Publishing Company

# UNIT 3 Measurement, Time, and Graphs

| BIG IDEA 1 | Length, Capacity, Weight and Mass |

| BIG IDEA 2 | Time and Date |

**Family Letter**

Dear Family,

In this unit and the next, your child will be practicing basic multiplications and divisions. *Math Expressions* incorporates studying, practicing, and testing of the basic multiplications and divisions in class. Your child is also expected to practice at home.

**Homework Helper** Your child will have math homework almost every day. He or she needs a Homework Helper. The helper may be anyone — you, an older brother or sister (or other family member), a neighbor, or a friend. Please decide who the main Homework Helper will be and ask your child to tell the teacher tomorrow. Make a specific time for homework and provide your child with a quiet place to work.

**Study Plans** Each day your child will fill out a study plan, indicating which basic multiplications and divisions he or she will study that evening. When your child has finished studying (practicing), his or her Homework Helper should sign the study plan.

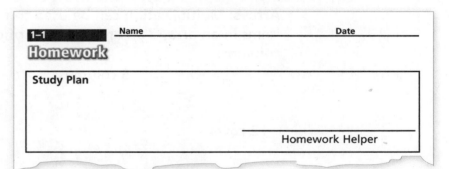

**Practice Charts** Each time a new number is introduced, students' homework will include a practice chart. To practice, students can cover the products with a pencil or a strip of heavy paper. They will say the multiplications, sliding the pencil or paper down the column to see each product after saying it. Students can also start with the last problem in a column and slide up. It is important that your child studies count-bys and multiplications at least 5 minutes every night. Your child can also use these charts to practice division on the mixed up column by covering the first factor.

| | In Order | Mixed Up |
|---|---|---|
| **5s** | 1 × 5 = 5 | 9 × 5 = 45 |
| | 2 × 5 = 10 | 5 × 5 = 25 |
| | 3 × 5 = 15 | 2 × 5 = 10 |
| | 4 × 5 = 20 | 7 × 5 = 35 |
| | 5 × 5 = 25 | 4 × 5 = 20 |
| | 6 × 5 = 30 | 6 × 5 = 30 |
| | 7 × 5 = 35 | 10 × 5 = 50 |
| | 8 × 5 = 40 | 8 × 5 = 40 |
| | 9 × 5 = 45 | 1 × 5 = 5 |
| | 10 × 5 = 50 | 3 × 5 = 15 |

Multiply with 5 **1**

To help students understand the concept of multiplication, the *Math Expressions* program presents three ways to think about multiplication.

- **Repeated groups**: Multiplication can be used to find the total in repeated groups of the same size. In early lessons, students circle the group size in repeated-groups equations to help keep track of which factor is the group size and which is the number of groups.

4 groups of bananas

$4 \times \textcircled{3} = 3 + 3 + 3 + 3 = 12$

- **Arrays**: Multiplication can be used to find the total number of items in an *array*—an arrangement of objects into rows and columns.

5 columns

2 rows                                          2-by-5 array

2 rows of pennies = $2 \times 5 = 10$

- **Area**: Multiplication can be used to find the area of a rectangle.

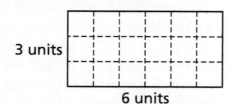

3 units

6 units

**Area**: 3 units × 6 units = 18 square units

Please call if you have any questions or comments.

Thank you.

Sincerely,
Your child's teacher

COMMON CORE   This unit includes the Common Core Standards for Mathematical Content for Operations and Algebraic Thinking, 3.OA.1, 3.OA.2, 3.OA.3, 3.OA.4, 3.OA.5, 3.OA.6, 3.OA.7, 3.OA.9, Measurement and Data, 3.MD.5a, 3.MD.5b, 3.MD.7a, 3.MD.7b, 3.MD.7c, 3.MD.7d, and all Mathematical Practices.

Carta a la familia

Estimada familia:

En esta unidad y en la que sigue, su niño practicará multiplicaciones y divisiones básicas. *Math Expressions* incorpora en la clase el estudio, la práctica y la evaluación de las multiplicaciones y divisiones básicas. También se espera que su niño practique en casa.

**Ayudante de tareas** Su niño tendrá tarea de matemáticas casi a diario y necesitará un ayudante para hacer sus tareas. Ese ayudante puede ser cualquier persona: usted, un hermano o hermana mayor, otro familiar, un vecino o un amigo. Por favor decida quién será esta persona y pida a su niño que se lo diga a su maestro mañana. Designe un tiempo específico para la tarea y un lugar para trabajar sin distracciones.

**Planes de estudio** Todos los días su niño va a completar un plan de estudio, que indica cuáles multiplicaciones y divisiones debe estudiar esa noche. Cuando su niño haya terminado de estudiar (practicar), la persona que lo ayude debe firmar el plan de estudio.

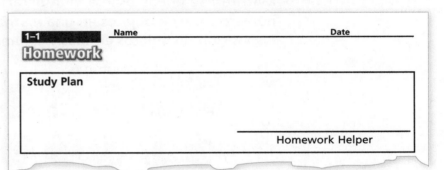

**Tablas de práctica** Cada vez que se presente un número nuevo, la tarea de los estudiantes incluirá una tabla de práctica. Para practicar, los estudiantes pueden cubrir los productos con un lápiz o una tira de papel grueso. Los niños dicen la multiplicación y deslizan el lápiz o el papel hacia abajo para revelar el producto después de decirlo. También pueden empezar con el último problema de la columna y deslizar el lápiz o el papel hacia arriba. Es importante que su niño practique el conteo y la multiplicación por lo menos 5 minutos cada noche. Su niño también puede usar estas tablas para practicar la división en la columna de productos desordenados cubriendo el primer factor.

| | En orden | Desordenados |
|---|---|---|
| | 1 × 5 = 5 | 9 × 5 = 45 |
| | 2 × 5 = 10 | 5 × 5 = 25 |
| | 3 × 5 = 15 | 2 × 5 = 10 |
| | 4 × 5 = 20 | 7 × 5 = 35 |
| **5** | 5 × 5 = 25 | 4 × 5 = 20 |
| | 6 × 5 = 30 | 6 × 5 = 30 |
| | 7 × 5 = 35 | 10 × 5 = 50 |
| | 8 × 5 = 40 | 8 × 5 = 40 |
| | 9 × 5 = 45 | 1 × 5 = 5 |
| | 10 × 5 = 50 | 3 × 5 = 15 |

**Para ayudar** a los estudiantes a comprender el concepto de la multiplicación, el programa *Math Expressions* presenta tres maneras de pensar en la multiplicación. Éstas se describen a continuación.

- **Grupos repetidos**: La multiplicación se puede usar para hallar el total con grupos del mismo tamaño que se repiten. Cuando empiezan a trabajar con ecuaciones de grupos repetidos, los estudiantes rodean con un círculo el tamaño del grupo en las ecuaciones, para recordar cuál factor representa el tamaño del grupo y cuál representa el número de grupos.

4 grupos de bananas
$4 \times ③ = 3 + 3 + 3 + 3 = 12$

- **Matrices**: Se puede usar la multiplicación para hallar el número total de objetos en una *matriz*, es decir, una disposición de objetos en filas y columnas.

5 columnas

2 filas                                            matriz de 2 por 5

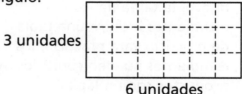

2 filas de monedas de un centavo = $2 \times 5 = 10$

- **Área**: Se puede usar la multiplicación para hallar el área de un rectángulo.

3 unidades

6 unidades

**Área**: 3 unidades $\times$ 6 unidades = 18 unidades cuadradas

Si tiene alguna duda o algún comentario, por favor comuníquese conmigo. Gracias.

Atentamente,
El maestro de su niño

**COMMON CORE** La Unidad 1 incluye los Common Core Standards for Mathematical Content for Operations and Algebraic Thinking, 3.OA.1, 3.OA.2, 3.OA.3, 3.OA.4, 3.OA.5, 3.OA.6, 3.OA.7, 3.OA.9, Measurement and Data, 3.MD.5a, 3.MD.5b, 3.MD.7a, 3.MD.7b, 3.MD.7c, 3.MD.7d, and all Mathematical Practices.

**Family Letter**

Dear Family,

In addition to practice charts for the basic multiplications and divisions for each of the numbers 1 through 10, your child will bring home a variety of other practice materials over the next several weeks.

- **Home Study Sheets:** A Home Study Sheet includes 3 or 4 practice charts on one page. Your child can use the Home Study Sheets to practice all the count-bys, multiplications, and divisions for a number or to practice just the ones he or she doesn't know for that number. The Homework Helper can then use the sheet to test (or retest) your child. The Homework Helper should check with your child to see which basic multiplications or divisions he or she is ready to be tested on. The helper should mark any missed problems lightly with a pencil.

If your child gets all the answers in a column correct, the helper should sign that column on the Home Signature Sheet. When signatures are on all the columns of the Home Signature Sheet, your child should bring the sheet to school.

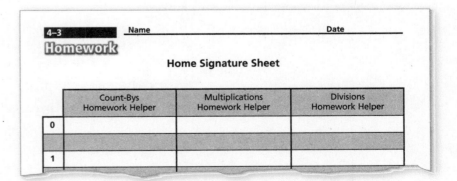

**Home Study Sheet A**

| 5s | | | 2s | | |
|---|---|---|---|---|---|
| **Count-bys** | **Mixed Up ×** | **Mixed Up ÷** | **Count-bys** | **Mixed Up ×** | **Mixed Up ÷** |
| 1 × 5 = 5 | 2 × 5 = 10 | 10 ÷ 5 = 2 | 1 × 2 = 2 | 7 × 2 = 14 | 20 ÷ 2 = 10 |
| 2 × 5 = 10 | 9 × 5 = 45 | 35 ÷ 5 = 7 | 2 × 2 = 4 | 1 × 2 = 2 | 2 ÷ 2 = 1 |
| 3 × 5 = 15 | 1 × 5 = 5 | 50 ÷ 5 = 10 | 3 × 2 = 6 | 3 × 2 = 6 | 6 ÷ 2 = 3 |
| 4 × 5 = 20 | 5 × 5 = 25 | 5 ÷ 5 = 1 | 4 × 2 = 8 | 5 × 2 = 10 | 16 ÷ 2 = 8 |
| 5 × 5 = 25 | 7 × 5 = 35 | 20 ÷ 5 = 4 | 5 × 2 = 10 | 6 × 2 = 12 | 12 ÷ 2 = 6 |
| 6 × 5 = 30 | 3 × 5 = 15 | 15 ÷ 5 = 3 | 6 × 2 = 12 | 8 × 2 = 16 | 4 ÷ 2 = 2 |
| 7 × 5 = 35 | 10 × 5 = 50 | 30 ÷ 5 = 6 | 7 × 2 = 14 | 2 × 2 = 4 | 10 ÷ 2 = 5 |
| 8 × 5 = 40 | 6 × 5 = 30 | 40 ÷ 5 = 8 | 8 × 2 = 16 | 10 × 2 = 20 | 8 ÷ 2 = 4 |
| 9 × 5 = 45 | 4 × 5 = 20 | 25 ÷ 5 = 5 | 9 × 2 = 18 | 4 × 2 = 8 | 14 ÷ 2 = 7 |
| 10 × 5 = 50 | 8 × 5 = 40 | 45 ÷ 5 = 9 | 10 × 2 = 20 | 9 × 2 = 18 | 18 ÷ 2 = 9 |

**4–3**

**Homework**

Name _____  Date _____

**Home Signature Sheet**

| | Count-Bys Homework Helper | Multiplications Homework Helper | Divisions Homework Helper |
|---|---|---|---|
| **0** | | | |
| | | | |
| **1** | | | |

- **Home Check Sheets:** A Home Check Sheet includes columns of 20 multiplications and divisions in mixed order. These sheets can be used to test your student's fluency with basic facts.

- **Strategy Cards:** Students use Strategy Cards in class as flashcards, to play games, and to develop multiplication and division strategies.

| **Sample Multiplication Card** | **Sample Division Card** |
| --- | --- |

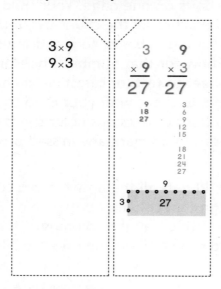 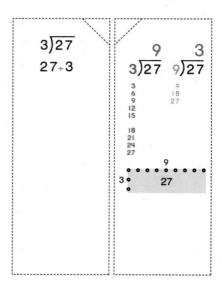

- **Games:** Near the end of this unit, students are introduced to games that provide multiplication and division practice.

Encourage your child to show you these materials and explain how they are used. Make sure your child spends time practicing multiplications and divisions every evening.

Please call if you have any questions or comments.

Thank you.

Sincerely,
Your child's teacher

 **COMMON CORE**  This unit includes the Common Core Standards for Mathematical Content for Operations and Algebraic Thinking, 3.OA.1, 3.OA.2, 3.OA.3, 3.OA.4, 3.OA.5, 3.OA.6, 3.OA.7, 3.OA.9, Measurement and Data, 3.MD.5a, 3.MD.5b, 3.MD.7a, 3.MD.7b, 3.MD.7c, 3.MD.7d, and all Mathematical Practices.

**Carta a la familia**

## Estimada familia:

Además de las tablas de práctica para las multiplicaciones y divisiones básicas para cada número del 1 al 10, su niño llevará a casa una variedad de materiales de práctica en las semanas que vienen.

- **Hojas para estudiar en casa:** Una hoja para estudiar en casa incluye 3 ó 4 tablas de práctica en una página. Su niño puede usar las hojas para practicar todos los conteos, multiplicaciones y divisiones de un número, o para practicar sólo las operaciones para ese número que no domine. La persona que ayude a su niño con la tarea puede usar la hoja para hacerle una prueba (o repetir una prueba). Esa persona debe hablar con su niño para decidir sobre qué multiplicaciones o divisiones básicas el niño puede hacer la prueba. La persona que ayude debe marcar ligeramente con un lápiz cualquier problema que conteste mal. Si su niño contesta bien todas las operaciones de una columna, la persona que ayude debe firmar esa columna de la hoja de firmas. Cuando todas las columnas de la hoja de firmas estén firmadas, su niño debe llevar la hoja a la escuela.

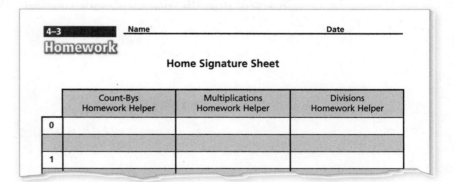

**Home Study Sheet A**

| 5s | | | 2s | | |
|---|---|---|---|---|---|
| Count-bys | Mixed Up × | Mixed Up ÷ | Count-bys | Mixed Up × | Mixed Up ÷ |
| 1 × 5 = 5 | 2 × 5 = 10 | 10 ÷ 5 = 2 | 1 × 2 = 2 | 7 × 2 = 14 | 20 ÷ 2 = 10 |
| 2 × 5 = 10 | 9 × 5 = 45 | 35 ÷ 5 = 7 | 2 × 2 = 4 | 1 × 2 = 2 | 2 ÷ 2 = 1 |
| 3 × 5 = 15 | 1 × 5 = 5 | 50 ÷ 5 = 10 | 3 × 2 = 6 | 3 × 2 = 6 | 6 ÷ 2 = 3 |
| 4 × 5 = 20 | 5 × 5 = 25 | 5 ÷ 5 = 1 | 4 × 2 = 8 | 5 × 2 = 10 | 16 ÷ 2 = 8 |
| 5 × 5 = 25 | 7 × 5 = 35 | 20 ÷ 5 = 4 | 5 × 2 = 10 | 6 × 2 = 12 | 12 ÷ 2 = 6 |
| 6 × 5 = 30 | 3 × 5 = 15 | 15 ÷ 5 = 3 | 6 × 2 = 12 | 8 × 2 = 16 | 4 ÷ 2 = 2 |
| 7 × 5 = 35 | 10 × 5 = 50 | 30 ÷ 5 = 6 | 7 × 2 = 14 | 2 × 2 = 4 | 10 ÷ 2 = 5 |
| 8 × 5 = 40 | 6 × 5 = 30 | 40 ÷ 5 = 8 | 8 × 2 = 16 | 10 × 2 = 20 | 8 ÷ 2 = 4 |
| 9 × 5 = 45 | 4 × 5 = 20 | 25 ÷ 5 = 5 | 9 × 2 = 18 | 4 × 2 = 8 | 14 ÷ 2 = 7 |
| 10 × 5 = 50 | 8 × 5 = 40 | 45 ÷ 5 = 9 | 10 × 2 = 20 | 9 × 2 = 18 | 18 ÷ 2 = 9 |

**4–3**

**Homework**

Name _____    Date _____

**Home Signature Sheet**

| | Count-Bys Homework Helper | Multiplications Homework Helper | Divisions Homework Helper |
|---|---|---|---|
| 0 | | | |
| 1 | | | |

© Houghton Mifflin Harcourt Publishing Company

• **Hojas de verificación:** Una hoja de verificación consta de columnas de 20 multiplicaciones y divisiones sin orden fijo. Estas hojas pueden usarse para comprobar el dominio de las operaciones básicas.

• **Tarjetas de estrategias:** Los estudiantes usan las tarjetas de estrategias en la clase como ayuda de memoria, en juegos y para desarrollar estrategias para hacer multiplicaciones y divisiones.

**Ejemplo de tarjeta de multiplicación**    **Ejemplo de tarjeta de división**

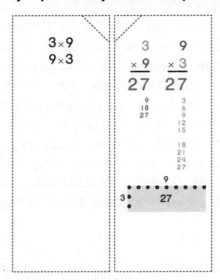
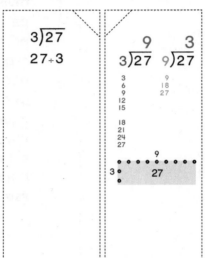

• **Juegos:** Hacia el final de esta unidad se presentan juegos a los estudiantes para practicar la multiplicación y la división.

Anime a su niño a que le muestre estos materiales y a que le explique cómo se usan. Asegúrese de que su niño practique la multiplicación y la división cada noche.

Si tiene alguna duda o pregunta, por favor comuníquese conmigo.

Atentamente,
El maestro de su niño

**COMMON CORE**

La Unidad 1 incluye los Common Core Standards for Mathematical Content for Operations and Algebraic Thinking, 3.OA.1, 3.OA.2, 3.OA.3, 3.OA.4, 3.OA.5, 3.OA.6, 3.OA.7, 3.OA.9, Measurement and Data, 3.MD.5a, 3.MD.5b, 3.MD.7a, 3.MD.7b, 3.MD.7c, 3.MD.7d, and all Mathematical Practices.

## Signature Sheet

| | Count-Bys Partner | Multiplications Partner | Divisions Partner | Multiplications Check Sheets | Divisions Check Sheets |
|---|---|---|---|---|---|
| **5s** | | | . | 1: | 1: |
| | | | | | |
| **2s** | | | | 1: | 1: |
| | | | | | |
| **10s** | | | | 2: | 2: |
| | | | | | |
| **9s** | | | | 2: | 2: |
| | | | | 3: | 3: |
| **3s** | | | | 4: | 4: |
| | | | | | |
| **4s** | | | | 4: | 4: |
| | | | | | |
| **1s** | | | | 5: | 5: |
| | | | | | |
| **0s** | | | | 5: | 5: |
| | | | | 6: | 6: |
| **6s** | | | | 7: | 7: |
| | | | | | |
| **8s** | | | | 7: | 7: |
| | | | | | |
| **7s** | | | | 8: | 8: |
| | | | | 9: | 9: |
| | | | | 10: | 10: |

Name _____     Date _____

## Dash Record Sheet

| Dash Number | Accurate | Fast | Really Fast |
|---|---|---|---|
| 1 | | | |
| 2 | | | |
| 3 | | | |
| 4 | | | |
| 5 | | | |
| 6 | | | |
| 7 | | | |
| 8 | | | |
| 9 | | | |
| 9A | | | |
| 9B | | | |
| 9C | | | |
| 10 | | | |
| 10A | | | |
| 10B | | | |
| 10C | | | |
| 11 | | | |
| 11A | | | |
| 11B | | | |
| 11C | | | |
| 12 | | | |
| 12A | | | |
| 12B | | | |
| 12C | | | |

| Dash Number | Accurate | Fast | Really Fast |
|---|---|---|---|
| 13 | | | |
| 14 | | | |
| 15 | | | |
| 16 | | | |
| 17 | | | |
| 18 | | | |
| 19 | | | |
| 19A | | | |
| 19B | | | |
| 19C | | | |
| 19D | | | |
| 20 | | | |
| 20A | | | |
| 20B | | | |
| 20C | | | |
| 20D | | | |
| 21 | | | |
| 21A | | | |
| 21B | | | |
| 21C | | | |
| 22 | | | |
| 22A | | | |
| 22B | | | |
| 22C | | | |

Dash Record Sheet

Name _____  Date _____

## Study Sheet A

### 5s

| Count-bys | Mixed Up × | Mixed Up ÷ |
|---|---|---|
| 1 × 5 = 5 | 2 × 5 = 10 | 10 ÷ 5 = 2 |
| 2 × 5 = 10 | 9 × 5 = 45 | 35 ÷ 5 = 7 |
| 3 × 5 = 15 | 1 × 5 = 5 | 50 ÷ 5 = 10 |
| 4 × 5 = 20 | 5 × 5 = 25 | 5 ÷ 5 = 1 |
| 5 × 5 = 25 | 7 × 5 = 35 | 20 ÷ 5 = 4 |
| 6 × 5 = 30 | 3 × 5 = 15 | 15 ÷ 5 = 3 |
| 7 × 5 = 35 | 10 × 5 = 50 | 30 ÷ 5 = 6 |
| 8 × 5 = 40 | 6 × 5 = 30 | 40 ÷ 5 = 8 |
| 9 × 5 = 45 | 4 × 5 = 20 | 25 ÷ 5 = 5 |
| 10 × 5 = 50 | 8 × 5 = 40 | 45 ÷ 5 = 9 |

### 2s

| Count-bys | Mixed Up × | Mixed Up ÷ |
|---|---|---|
| 1 × 2 = 2 | 7 × 2 = 14 | 20 ÷ 2 = 10 |
| 2 × 2 = 4 | 1 × 2 = 2 | 2 ÷ 2 = 1 |
| 3 × 2 = 6 | 3 × 2 = 6 | 6 ÷ 2 = 3 |
| 4 × 2 = 8 | 5 × 2 = 10 | 16 ÷ 2 = 8 |
| 5 × 2 = 10 | 6 × 2 = 12 | 12 ÷ 2 = 6 |
| 6 × 2 = 12 | 8 × 2 = 16 | 4 ÷ 2 = 2 |
| 7 × 2 = 14 | 2 × 2 = 4 | 10 ÷ 2 = 5 |
| 8 × 2 = 16 | 10 × 2 = 20 | 8 ÷ 2 = 4 |
| 9 × 2 = 18 | 4 × 2 = 8 | 14 ÷ 2 = 7 |
| 10 × 2 = 20 | 9 × 2 = 18 | 18 ÷ 2 = 9 |

### 10s

| Count-bys | Mixed Up × | Mixed Up ÷ |
|---|---|---|
| 1 × 10 = 10 | 1 × 10 = 10 | 80 ÷ 10 = 8 |
| 2 × 10 = 20 | 5 × 10 = 50 | 10 ÷ 10 = 1 |
| 3 × 10 = 30 | 2 × 10 = 20 | 50 ÷ 10 = 5 |
| 4 × 10 = 40 | 8 × 10 = 80 | 90 ÷ 10 = 9 |
| 5 × 10 = 50 | 7 × 10 = 70 | 40 ÷ 10 = 4 |
| 6 × 10 = 60 | 3 × 10 = 30 | 100 ÷ 10 = 10 |
| 7 × 10 = 70 | 4 × 10 = 40 | 30 ÷ 10 = 3 |
| 8 × 10 = 80 | 6 × 10 = 60 | 20 ÷ 10 = 2 |
| 9 × 10 = 90 | 10 × 10 = 100 | 70 ÷ 10 = 7 |
| 10 × 10 = 100 | 9 × 10 = 90 | 60 ÷ 10 = 6 |

### 9s

| Count-bys | Mixed Up × | Mixed Up ÷ |
|---|---|---|
| 1 × 9 = 9 | 2 × 9 = 18 | 81 ÷ 9 = 9 |
| 2 × 9 = 18 | 4 × 9 = 36 | 18 ÷ 9 = 2 |
| 3 × 9 = 27 | 7 × 9 = 63 | 36 ÷ 9 = 4 |
| 4 × 9 = 36 | 8 × 9 = 72 | 9 ÷ 9 = 1 |
| 5 × 9 = 45 | 3 × 9 = 27 | 54 ÷ 9 = 6 |
| 6 × 9 = 54 | 10 × 9 = 90 | 27 ÷ 9 = 3 |
| 7 × 9 = 63 | 1 × 9 = 9 | 63 ÷ 9 = 7 |
| 8 × 9 = 72 | 6 × 9 = 54 | 72 ÷ 9 = 8 |
| 9 × 9 = 81 | 5 × 9 = 45 | 90 ÷ 9 = 10 |
| 10 × 9 = 90 | 9 × 9 = 81 | 45 ÷ 9 = 5 |

Study Sheet A

► PATH to FLUENCY **Use the Target**

| ×  | 0 | 1 | 2  | 3  | 4  | 5  | 6  | 7  | 8  | 9  |
|----|---|---|----|----|----|----|----|----|----|----|
| 0  | 0 | 0 | 0  | 0  | 0  | 0  | 0  | 0  | 0  | 0  |
| 1  | 0 | 1 | 2  | 3  | 4  | 5  | 6  | 7  | 8  | 9  |
| 2  | 0 | 2 | 4  | 6  | 8  | 10 | 12 | 14 | 16 | 18 |
| 3  | 0 | 3 | 6  | 9  | 12 | 15 | 18 | 21 | 24 | 27 |
| 4  | 0 | 4 | 8  | 12 | 16 | 20 | 24 | 28 | 32 | 36 |
| 5  | 0 | 5 | 10 | 15 | 20 | 25 | 30 | 35 | 40 | 45 |
| 6  | 0 | 6 | 12 | 18 | 24 | 30 | 36 | 42 | 48 | 54 |
| 7  | 0 | 7 | 14 | 21 | 28 | 35 | 42 | 49 | 56 | 63 |
| 8  | 0 | 8 | 16 | 24 | 32 | 40 | 48 | 56 | 64 | 72 |
| 9  | 0 | 9 | 18 | 27 | 36 | 45 | 54 | 63 | 72 | 81 |

1. Discuss how you can use the Target to find the product for $8 \times 5$.

2. Discuss how you can use the Target to practice division.

3. Practice using the Target.

4. When using the Target, how are multiplication and division alike? How are they different?

_____

_____

_____

_____

## ► Make Sense of Problems

**Write an equation and solve the problem.**

*Show your work.*

5. Mrs. Cheng bought 8 pairs of mittens. How many individual mittens did she buy?

_____

6. Brian divided 10 crayons equally between his two sisters. How many crayons did each girl get?

_____

7. Maria has 5 piles of flash cards. There are 9 cards in each pile. How many flash cards does Maria have?

_____

8. A parking lot has 5 rows of parking spaces with the same number of spaces in each row. There are 35 parking spaces in the lot. How many spaces are in each row?

_____

9. Ari arranged his bottle cap collection into 9 rows with 2 bottle caps in each row. How many bottle caps are in his collection?

_____

## ► Write a Word Problem

10. Write a word problem that can be solved using the equation $45 \div 5 =$ where 5 is the number of groups.

_____

_____

_____

VOCABULARY
equation
variable

## ▶ Use Variables in Equations

When you write **equations** you can use a letter to represent an unknown number. This letter is called a **variable**.

Each of these equations has a variable.

| | | | |
|---|---|---|---|
| $a \times 10 = 60$ | $70 = c \times 7$ | $w = 80 \div 10$ | $9 = 90 \div c$ |
| $2 \times y = 18$ | $p = 9 \times 2$ | $f = 18 \div 2$ | $18 \div n = 2$ |

**Solve each equation.**

7. $14 = 7 \times a$

$a =$ _____

8. $90 \div g = 9$

$g =$ _____

9. $10 \div n = 5$

$n =$ _____

10. $8 \times f = 40$

$f =$ _____

## ▶ Write and Solve Equations with Variables

**Write an equation and solve the problem.**

11. A box of straws holds 60 straws. There are 10 straws in each row. How many rows are there?

_____

12. Ethan used 9 dimes to pay for his book. How much did his book cost?

_____

13. There are 10 relay teams with an equal number of people on each team running a race. There are 50 people running the race. How many people are there on each team?

_____

14. Amanda has 20 bracelets. She gave the same number of bracelets to 2 of her friends. How many bracelets did she give to each friend?

_____

## ▶ What's the Error?

Dear Math Students,

Today my teacher asked me to write a word
problem that can be solved using the division
40 ÷ 10. Here is the problem I wrote:

　　Kim has 40 apples and puts 4 apples in
　　each bag. How many bags did Kim use?

Is my problem correct? If not, please correct
my work and tell me what I did wrong.

Your friend,
Puzzled Penguin

**15. Write an answer to the Puzzled Penguin.**

_____

_____

_____

## ▶ Write and Solve Problems with 10s

16. Write a word problem that can be solved using the division 60 ÷ 10.
Then write a related multiplication word problem.

_____

_____

17. Write a word problem that can be solved using the multiplication
10 × 3. Then write a related division word problem.

_____

_____

**Name** _____  **Date** _____

► PATH to FLUENCY  **Check Sheet 2: 10s and 9s**

| 10s Multiplications | 10s Divisions | 9s Multiplications | 9s Divisions |
|---|---|---|---|
| 9 × 10 = 90 | 100 / 10 = 10 | 3 × 9 = 27 | 27 / 9 = 3 |
| 10 • 3 = 30 | 50 ÷ 10 = 5 | 9 • 7 = 63 | 9 ÷ 9 = 1 |
| 10 * 6 = 60 | 70 / 10 = 7 | 10 * 9 = 90 | 81 / 9 = 9 |
| 1 × 10 = 10 | 40 ÷ 10 = 4 | 5 × 9 = 45 | 45 ÷ 9 = 5 |
| 10 • 4 = 40 | 80 / 10 = 8 | 9 • 8 = 72 | 90 / 9 = 10 |
| 10 * 7 = 70 | 60 ÷ 10 = 6 | 9 * 1 = 9 | 36 ÷ 9 = 4 |
| 8 × 10 = 80 | 10 / 10 = 1 | 2 × 9 = 18 | 18 / 9 = 2 |
| 10 • 10 = 100 | 20 ÷ 10 = 2 | 9 • 9 = 81 | 63 ÷ 9 = 7 |
| 5 * 10 = 50 | 90 / 10 = 9 | 6 * 9 = 54 | 54 / 9 = 6 |
| 10 × 2 = 20 | 30 / 10 = 3 | 9 × 4 = 36 | 72 / 9 = 8 |
| 10 • 5 = 50 | 80 ÷ 10 = 8 | 9 • 5 = 45 | 27 ÷ 9 = 3 |
| 4 * 10 = 40 | 70 / 10 = 7 | 4 * 9 = 36 | 45 / 9 = 5 |
| 10 × 1 = 10 | 100 ÷ 10 = 10 | 9 × 1 = 9 | 63 ÷ 9 = 7 |
| 3 • 10 = 30 | 90 / 10 = 9 | 3 • 9 = 27 | 72 / 9 = 8 |
| 10 * 8 = 80 | 60 ÷ 10 = 6 | 9 * 8 = 72 | 54 ÷ 9 = 6 |
| 7 × 10 = 70 | 30 / 10 = 3 | 7 × 9 = 63 | 18 / 9 = 2 |
| 6 • 10 = 60 | 10 ÷ 10 = 1 | 6 • 9 = 54 | 90 ÷ 9 = 10 |
| 10 * 9 = 90 | 40 ÷ 10 = 4 | 9 * 9 = 81 | 9 ÷ 9 = 1 |
| 10 × 10 = 100 | 20 / 10 = 2 | 10 × 9 = 90 | 36 / 9 = 4 |
| 2 • 10 = 20 | 50 ÷ 10 = 5 | 2 • 9 = 18 | 81 ÷ 9 = 9 |

Check Sheet 2: 10s and 9s

► PATH to FLUENCY **Explore Patterns with 9s**

## What patterns do you see below?

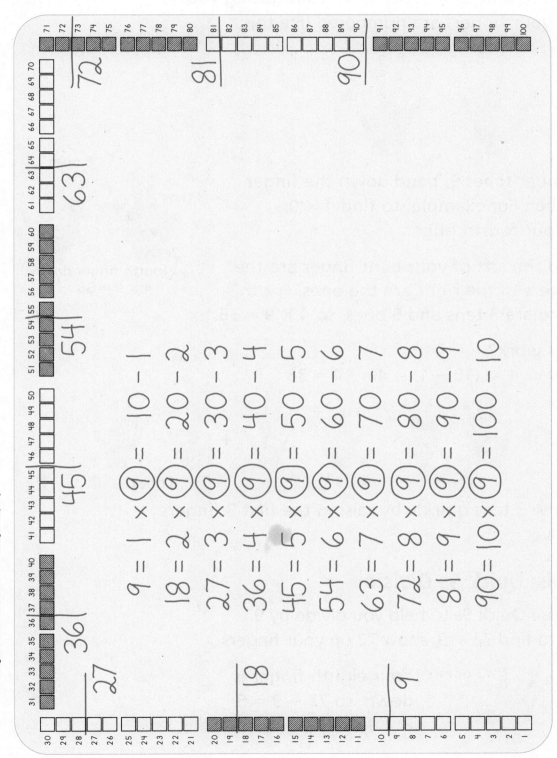

$$9 = 1 \times 9 = 10 - 1$$
$$18 = 2 \times 9 = 20 - 2$$
$$27 = 3 \times 9 = 30 - 3$$
$$36 = 4 \times 9 = 40 - 4$$
$$45 = 5 \times 9 = 50 - 5$$
$$54 = 6 \times 9 = 60 - 6$$
$$63 = 7 \times 9 = 70 - 7$$
$$72 = 8 \times 9 = 80 - 8$$
$$81 = 9 \times 9 = 90 - 9$$
$$90 = 10 \times 9 = 100 - 10$$

## ▶ Math Tools: Quick 9s Multiplication

You can use the Quick 9s method to help you multiply by 9. Open your hands and turn them so they are facing you. Imagine that your fingers are numbered like this.

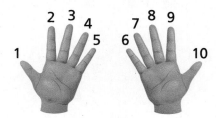

To find a number times 9, bend down the finger for that number. For example, to find $4 \times 9$, bend down your fourth finger.

The fingers to the left of your bent finger are the tens. The fingers to the right are the ones. For this problem, there are 3 tens and 6 ones, so $4 \times 9 = 36$.

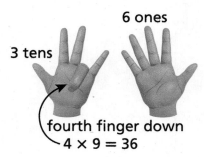

6 ones

3 tens

fourth finger down
$4 \times 9 = 36$

Why does this work?
Because $4 \times 9 = 4 \times (10 - 1) = 40 - 4 = 36$

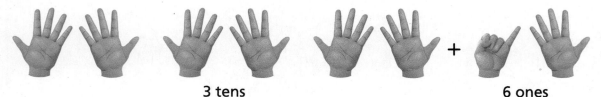

3 tens          + 6 ones

You could show 3 tens quickly by raising the first 3 fingers as shown above.

## ▶ Math Tools: Quick 9s Division

You can also use Quick 9s to help you divide by 9. For example, to find $72 \div 9$, show 72 on your fingers.

7 tens          2 ones

Your eighth finger is down, so $72 \div 9 = 8$.
$8 \times 9 = 80 - 8 = 72$

► **PATH to FLUENCY** **Check Sheet 3: 2s, 5s, 9s, and 10s**

| 2s, 5s, 9s, 10s Multiplications | 2s, 5s, 9s, 10s Multiplications | 2s, 5s, 9s, 10s Divisions | 2s, 5s, 9s, 10s Divisions |
|---|---|---|---|
| $2 \times 10 = 20$ | $5 \times 10 = 50$ | $18 / 2 = 9$ | $36 / 9 = 4$ |
| $10 \cdot 5 = 50$ | $10 \cdot 9 = 90$ | $50 \div 5 = 10$ | $70 \div 10 = 7$ |
| $9 * 6 = 54$ | $4 * 10 = 40$ | $72 / 9 = 8$ | $18 / 2 = 9$ |
| $7 \times 10 = 70$ | $2 \times 9 = 18$ | $60 \div 10 = 6$ | $45 \div 5 = 9$ |
| $2 \cdot 3 = 6$ | $5 \cdot 3 = 15$ | $12 / 2 = 6$ | $45 / 9 = 5$ |
| $5 * 7 = 35$ | $6 * 9 = 54$ | $30 \div 5 = 6$ | $30 \div 10 = 3$ |
| $9 \times 10 = 90$ | $10 \times 3 = 30$ | $18 / 9 = 2$ | $6 / 2 = 3$ |
| $6 \cdot 10 = 60$ | $3 \cdot 2 = 6$ | $50 \div 10 = 5$ | $50 \div 5 = 10$ |
| $8 * 2 = 16$ | $5 * 8 = 40$ | $14 / 2 = 7$ | $27 / 9 = 3$ |
| $5 \times 6 = 30$ | $9 \times 9 = 81$ | $25 / 5 = 5$ | $70 / 10 = 7$ |
| $9 \cdot 5 = 45$ | $10 \cdot 4 = 40$ | $81 \div 9 = 9$ | $20 \div 2 = 10$ |
| $8 * 10 = 80$ | $9 * 2 = 18$ | $20 / 10 = 2$ | $45 / 5 = 9$ |
| $2 \times 1 = 2$ | $5 \times 1 = 5$ | $8 \div 2 = 4$ | $54 \div 9 = 6$ |
| $3 \cdot 5 = 15$ | $9 \cdot 6 = 54$ | $45 / 5 = 9$ | $80 / 10 = 8$ |
| $4 * 9 = 36$ | $10 * 1 = 10$ | $63 \div 9 = 7$ | $16 \div 2 = 8$ |
| $3 \times 10 = 30$ | $7 \times 2 = 14$ | $30 / 10 = 3$ | $15 / 5 = 3$ |
| $2 \cdot 6 = 12$ | $6 \cdot 5 = 30$ | $10 \div 2 = 5$ | $90 \div 9 = 10$ |
| $4 * 5 = 20$ | $8 * 9 = 72$ | $40 \div 5 = 8$ | $100 \div 10 = 10$ |
| $9 \times 7 = 63$ | $10 \times 6 = 60$ | $9 / 9 = 1$ | $12 / 2 = 6$ |
| $1 \cdot 10 = 10$ | $2 \cdot 8 = 16$ | $50 \div 10 = 5$ | $35 \div 5 = 7$ |

Check Sheet 3: 2s, 5s, 9s, and 10s

## ▶ Make Sense of Problems with 2s, 5s, 9s, and 10s

**Write an equation to represent each problem. Then solve the problem.**

*Show your work.*

1. Ian planted tulip bulbs in an array with 5 rows and 10 columns. How many bulbs did he plant?

   _____

2. Erin gave 30 basketball cards to her 5 cousins. Each cousin got the same number of cards. How many cards did each cousin get?

   _____

3. Martina bought 7 cans of racquetballs. There were 2 balls per can. How many racquetballs did she buy in all?

   _____

4. The 27 students in the orchestra stood in rows for their school picture. There were 9 students in every row. How many rows of students were there?

   _____

5. Lindsey needs 40 note cards. The note cards are packaged 10 to a box. How many boxes of cards should Lindsey buy?

   _____

6. There are 25 student desks in the classroom. The desks are arranged in 5 rows with the same number of desks in each row. How many desks are in each row?

   _____

Name _____ Date _____

# ► Math Tools: Fast Array Drawings

When you solve a word problem involving an array, you can save time by making a Fast Array drawing. This type of drawing shows the number of items in each row and column, but does not show every single item.

**Here is how you might use a Fast Array drawing for problem 1 on Student Activity Book page 43.**

Show the number of rows and the number of columns. Make a box in the center to show that you don't know the total.

Here are three ways to find the total.

- Find $5 \times 10$.
- Use 10s count-bys to find the total in 5 rows of 10: 10, 20, 30, 40, 50.
- Use 5s count-bys to find the total in 10 rows of 5: 5, 10, 15, 20, 25, 30, 35, 40, 45, 50.

**Here is how you might use a Fast Array drawing for problem 4 on page 43.**

Show the number in each row and the total. Make a box to show that you don't know the number of rows.

Here are two ways to find the number of rows.

- Find $27 \div 9$ or solve $\square \times 9 = 27$.
- Count by 9s until you reach 27: 9, 18, 27.

**Math Journal** **Make a Fast Array drawing to solve each problem.**

7. Beth planted tulip bulbs in an array with 9 rows and 6 columns. How many bulbs did she plant?

8. The 36 students in the chorus stood in 4 rows for their school picture. How many students were in each row?

Building Fluency with 2s, 5s, 9s, and 10s

| $2 \times 2$ | $\begin{array}{r} 2 \\ \times 3 \end{array}$ $\begin{array}{r} 3 \\ \times 2 \end{array}$ | $\begin{array}{r} 2 \times 4 \\ 4 \times 2 \end{array}$ | $\begin{array}{r} 2 \\ \times 5 \end{array}$ $\begin{array}{r} 5 \\ \times 2 \end{array}$ |
|---|---|---|---|
| $\begin{array}{r} 2 \times 6 \\ 6 \times 2 \end{array}$ | $\begin{array}{r} 2 \\ \times 7 \end{array}$ $\begin{array}{r} 7 \\ \times 2 \end{array}$ | $\begin{array}{r} 2 \times 8 \\ 8 \times 2 \end{array}$ | $\begin{array}{r} 2 \\ \times 9 \end{array}$ $\begin{array}{r} 9 \\ \times 2 \end{array}$ |

**Card 1:**

$10 = 2 \times 5$

$10 = 5 \times 2$

```
5    2
10   4
     6
     8
     10
```

2 | 5 ... 10

**Card 2:**

$2 \times 4 = 8$   $4 \times 2 = 8$

```
2      4
8      8
2      
4      
6      
8      
```

2, 4 | 8

**Card 3:**

$6 = 2 \times 3$

$6 = 3 \times 2$

```
3    2
6    4
     6
```

2 | 3 ... 6

**Card 4:**

$2 \times 2 = 4$

```
2
4
```

2 | 2 ... 4

**Card 5:**

$18 = 2 \times 9$

$18 = 9 \times 2$

```
9      2
18     4
       6
       8
       10

       12
       14
       16
       18
```

2 | 9 ... 18

**Card 6:**

$2 \times 8 = 16$   $8 \times 2 = 16$

```
8      2
16     4
       6
       8
       10

       12
       14
       16
```

2, 8 | 16

**Card 7:**

$14 = 2 \times 7$

$14 = 7 \times 2$

```
7      2
14     4
       6
       8
       10

       12
       14
```

2 | 7 ... 14

**Card 8:**

$2 \times 6 = 12$   $6 \times 2 = 12$

```
6      2
12     4
       6
       8
       10

       12
```

2, 6 | 12

Multiplication Strategy Cards

$3 \times 3$

$$\begin{array}{r} 3 \\ \times\ 4 \\ \hline \end{array} \qquad \begin{array}{r} 4 \\ \times\ 3 \\ \hline \end{array}$$

$3 \times 5$
$5 \times 3$

$$\begin{array}{r} 3 \\ \times\ 6 \\ \hline \end{array} \qquad \begin{array}{r} 6 \\ \times\ 3 \\ \hline \end{array}$$

$3 \times 7$
$7 \times 3$

$$\begin{array}{r} 3 \\ \times\ 8 \\ \hline \end{array} \qquad \begin{array}{r} 8 \\ \times\ 3 \\ \hline \end{array}$$

$3 \times 9$
$9 \times 3$

$$\begin{array}{r} 4 \\ \times\ 4 \\ \hline \end{array}$$

## Card 1

$18 = 3 \times 6$

$18 = 6 \times 3$

| 6 | 3 |
|---|---|
| 12 | 6 |
| 18 | 9 |
| | 12 |
| | 15 |
| | 18 |

6

3 ○ 18

## Card 2

$\times \dfrac{5}{15}$  $\times \dfrac{5}{15}$

(top: 3   5)

| 5 | 3 |
|---|---|
| 10 | 6 |
| 15 | 9 |
| | 12 |
| | 15 |

3

5 ○ 15

## Card 3

$12 = 3 \times 4$

$12 = 4 \times 3$

| 4 | 3 |
|---|---|
| 8 | 6 |
| 12 | 9 |
| | 12 |

4

3 ○ 12

## Card 4

(top: 3)

$\times \dfrac{3}{9}$

| 3 |
|---|
| 6 |
| 9 |

3

3 ○ 9

## Card 5

$16 = 4 \times 4$

| 4 |
|---|
| 8 |
| 12 |
| 16 |

4

4 ○ 16

## Card 6

(top: 3   9)

$\times \dfrac{9}{27}$  $\times \dfrac{3}{27}$

| 9 | 3 |
|---|---|
| 18 | 6 |
| 27 | 9 |
| | 12 |
| | 15 |
| | 18 |
| | 21 |
| | 24 |
| | 27 |

9

3 ○ 27

## Card 7

$24 = 3 \times 8$

$24 = 8 \times 3$

| 8 | 3 |
|---|---|
| 16 | 6 |
| 24 | 9 |
| | 12 |
| | 15 |
| | 18 |
| | 21 |
| | 24 |

3

8 ○ 24

## Card 8

(top: 3   7)

$\times \dfrac{7}{21}$  $\times \dfrac{3}{21}$

| 7 | 3 |
|---|---|
| 14 | 6 |
| 21 | 9 |
| | 12 |
| | 15 |
| | 18 |
| | 21 |

7

3 ○ 21

Multiplication Strategy Cards

$4 \times 5$
$5 \times 4$

$\begin{array}{r} 4 \\ \times 6 \end{array}$  $\begin{array}{r} 6 \\ \times 4 \end{array}$

$4 \times 7$
$7 \times 4$

$\begin{array}{r} 4 \\ \times 8 \end{array}$  $\begin{array}{r} 8 \\ \times 4 \end{array}$

$4 \times 9$
$9 \times 4$

$\begin{array}{r} 5 \\ \times 5 \end{array}$

$5 \times 6$
$6 \times 5$

$\begin{array}{r} 5 \\ \times 7 \end{array}$  $\begin{array}{r} 7 \\ \times 5 \end{array}$

Multiplication Strategy Cards **51E**

## Card 1

$$32 = 4 \times 8$$
$$32 = 8 \times 4$$

| 8 | 4 |
|---|---|
| 16 | 8 |
| 24 | 12 |
| 32 | 16 |
| | 20 |
| | 24 |
| | 28 |
| | 32 |

4

8 | 32

## Card 2

$$\begin{array}{r} 4 \\ \times 7 \\ \hline 28 \end{array} \qquad \begin{array}{r} 7 \\ \times 4 \\ \hline 28 \end{array}$$

| 7 | 4 |
|---|---|
| 14 | 8 |
| 21 | 12 |
| 28 | 16 |
| | 20 |
| | 24 |
| | 28 |

7

4 | 28

## Card 3

$$24 = 4 \times 6$$
$$24 = 6 \times 4$$

| 6 | 4 |
|---|---|
| 12 | 8 |
| 18 | 12 |
| 24 | 16 |
| | 20 |
| | 24 |

4

6 | 24

## Card 4

$$\begin{array}{r} 4 \\ \times 5 \\ \hline 20 \end{array} \qquad \begin{array}{r} 5 \\ \times 4 \\ \hline 20 \end{array}$$

| 5 | 4 |
|---|---|
| 10 | 8 |
| 15 | 12 |
| 20 | 16 |
| | 20 |

5

4 | 20

## Card 5

$$35 = 5 \times 7$$
$$35 = 7 \times 5$$

| 7 | 5 |
|---|---|
| 14 | 10 |
| 21 | 15 |
| 28 | 20 |
| 35 | 25 |
| | 30 |
| | 35 |

7

5 | 35

## Card 6

$$\begin{array}{r} 5 \\ \times 6 \\ \hline 30 \end{array} \qquad \begin{array}{r} 6 \\ \times 5 \\ \hline 30 \end{array}$$

| 6 | 5 |
|---|---|
| 12 | 10 |
| 18 | 15 |
| 24 | 20 |
| 30 | 25 |
| | 30 |

5

6 | 30

## Card 7

$$25 = 5 \times 5$$

| 5 |
|---|
| 10 |
| 15 |
| 20 |
| 25 |

5

5 | 25

## Card 8

$$\begin{array}{r} 4 \\ \times 9 \\ \hline 36 \end{array} \qquad \begin{array}{r} 9 \\ \times 4 \\ \hline 36 \end{array}$$

| 9 | 4 |
|---|---|
| 18 | 8 |
| 27 | 12 |
| 36 | 16 |
| | 20 |
| | 24 |
| | 28 |
| | 32 |
| | 36 |

9

4 | 36

$5 \times 8$
$8 \times 5$

$$\begin{array}{r} 5 \\ \times 9 \end{array} \qquad \begin{array}{r} 9 \\ \times 5 \end{array}$$

$6 \times 6$

$$\begin{array}{r} 6 \\ \times 7 \end{array} \qquad \begin{array}{r} 7 \\ \times 6 \end{array}$$

$6 \times 8$
$8 \times 6$

$$\begin{array}{r} 6 \\ \times 9 \end{array} \qquad \begin{array}{r} 9 \\ \times 6 \end{array}$$

$7 \times 7$

$$\begin{array}{r} 7 \\ \times 8 \end{array} \qquad \begin{array}{r} 8 \\ \times 7 \end{array}$$

# Multiplication Strategy Cards

## Card 1
$42 = 7 \times 6$
$42 = 6 \times 7$

| 6 | 7 |
|---|---|
| 12 | 14 |
| 18 | 21 |
| 24 | 28 |
| 30 | 35 |
| 36 | 42 |
| 42 | |

7
6 → 42

## Card 2
$\begin{array}{r} 6 \\ \times 6 \\ \hline 36 \end{array}$

6
12
18
24
30

36

6
6 → 36

## Card 3
$45 = 9 \times 5$
$45 = 5 \times 9$

| 5 | 9 |
|---|---|
| 10 | 18 |
| 15 | 27 |
| 20 | 36 |
| 25 | 45 |
| 30 | |
| 35 | |
| 40 | |
| 45 | |

9
5 → 45

## Card 4
$\begin{array}{r} 8 \\ \times 5 \\ \hline 40 \end{array}$    $\begin{array}{r} 5 \\ \times 8 \\ \hline 40 \end{array}$

| 5 | 8 |
|---|---|
| 10 | 16 |
| 15 | 24 |
| 20 | 32 |
| 25 | 40 |
| 30 | |
| 35 | |
| 40 | |

5
8 → 40

## Card 5
$56 = 7 \times 8$
$56 = 8 \times 7$

| 8 | 7 |
|---|---|
| 16 | 14 |
| 24 | 21 |
| 32 | 28 |
| 40 | 35 |
| 48 | 42 |
| 56 | 49 |
| | 56 |

8
7 → 56

## Card 6
$\begin{array}{r} 7 \\ \times 7 \\ \hline 49 \end{array}$

7
14
21
28
35

42
49

7
7 → 49

## Card 7
$54 = 9 \times 6$
$54 = 6 \times 9$

| 6 | 9 |
|---|---|
| 12 | 18 |
| 18 | 27 |
| 24 | 36 |
| 30 | 45 |
| 36 | 54 |
| 42 | |
| 48 | |
| 54 | |

9
6 → 54

## Card 8
$\begin{array}{r} 6 \\ \times 8 \\ \hline 48 \end{array}$    $\begin{array}{r} 8 \\ \times 6 \\ \hline 48 \end{array}$

| 6 | 8 |
|---|---|
| 12 | 16 |
| 18 | 24 |
| 24 | 32 |
| 30 | 40 |
| 36 | 48 |
| 42 | |
| 48 | |

8
6 → 48

Multiplication Strategy Cards

7×9
9×7

8
× 8

9×8
8×9

9
× 9

## Card 1

$81 = 9 \times 9$

9
18
27
36
45

54
63
72
81

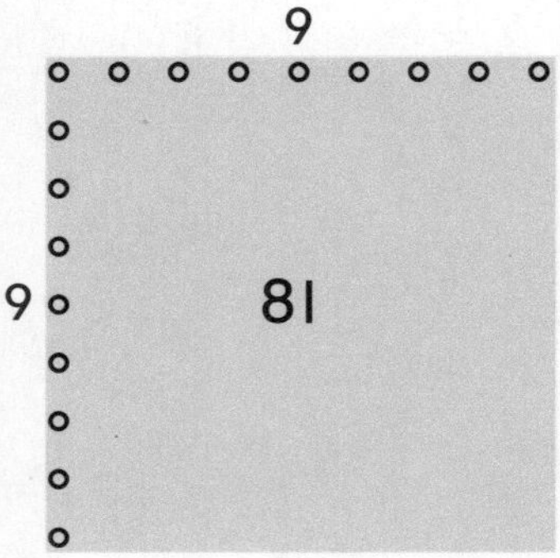

9

81

9

## Card 2

$$\begin{array}{r} 9 \\ \times\ 8 \\ \hline 72 \end{array} \qquad \begin{array}{r} 8 \\ \times\ 9 \\ \hline 72 \end{array}$$

| 8 | 9 |
|---|---|
| 16 | 18 |
| 24 | 27 |
| 32 | 36 |
| 40 | 45 |
| | |
| 48 | 54 |
| 56 | 63 |
| 64 | 72 |
| 72 | |

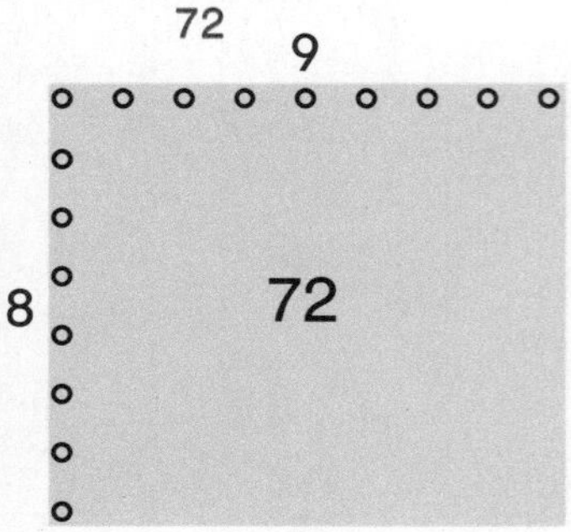

9

72

8

## Card 3

$64 = 8 \times 8$

8
16
24
32
40

48
56
64

8

64

8

## Card 4

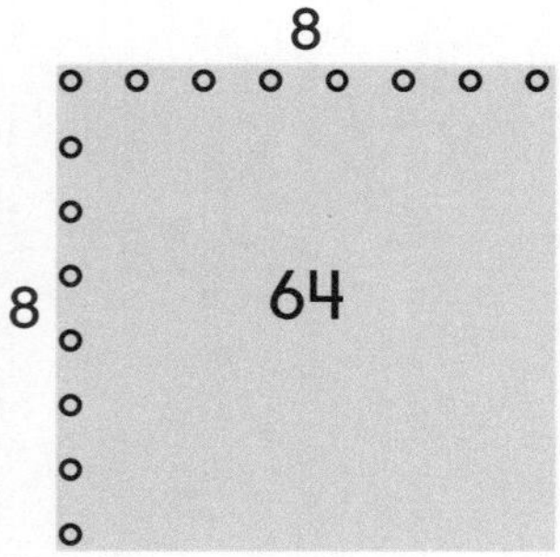

$$\begin{array}{r} 7 \\ \times\ 9 \\ \hline 63 \end{array} \qquad \begin{array}{r} 9 \\ \times\ 7 \\ \hline 63 \end{array}$$

| 9 | 7 |
|---|---|
| 18 | 14 |
| 27 | 21 |
| 36 | 28 |
| 45 | 35 |
| | |
| 54 | 42 |
| 63 | 49 |
| | 56 |
| | 63 |

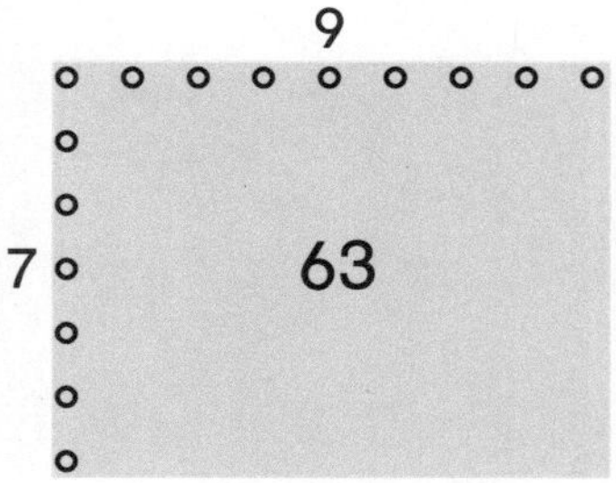

9

63

7

Multiplication Strategy Cards

$2\overline{)4}$

$4 \div 2$

$2\overline{)6}$

$6 \div 2$

$2\overline{)8}$

$8 \div 2$

$2\overline{)10}$

$10 \div 2$

$2\overline{)12}$

$12 \div 2$

$2\overline{)14}$

$14 \div 2$

$2\overline{)16}$

$16 \div 2$

$2\overline{)18}$

$18 \div 2$

## Card 1

$$5 \quad 2$$

$2\overline{)10} \quad 5\overline{)10}$

2   5
4   10
6
8
10

5
2 · 10

## Card 2

$$4 \quad 2$$

$2\overline{)8} \quad 4\overline{)8}$

2   4
4   8
6
8

4
2 · 8

## Card 3

$$3 \quad 2$$

$2\overline{)6} \quad 3\overline{)6}$

2   3
4   6
6

3
2 · 6

## Card 4

$$2$$

$2\overline{)4}$

2
4

2
2 · 4

## Card 5

$$9 \quad 2$$

$2\overline{)18} \quad 9\overline{)18}$

2   9
4   18
6
8
10

12
14
16
18

9
2 · 18

## Card 6

$$8 \quad 2$$

$2\overline{)16} \quad 8\overline{)16}$

2   8
4   16
6
8
10

12
14
16

8
2 · 16

## Card 7

$$7 \quad 2$$

$2\overline{)14} \quad 7\overline{)14}$

2   7
4   14
6
8
10

12
14

7
2 · 14

## Card 8

$$6 \quad 2$$

$2\overline{)12} \quad 6\overline{)12}$

2   6
4   12
6
8
10

12

6
2 · 12

**51L** UNIT 1 LESSON 11
© Houghton Mifflin Harcourt Publishing Company

Division Strategy Cards

$3 \overline{)6}$

$6 \div 3$

$4 \overline{)8}$

$8 \div 4$

$5 \overline{)10}$

$10 \div 5$

$6 \overline{)12}$

$12 \div 6$

$7 \overline{)14}$

$14 \div 7$

$8 \overline{)16}$

$16 \div 8$

$9 \overline{)18}$

$18 \div 9$

$3 \overline{)9}$

$9 \div 3$

## Card 1

$$6\overline{)12} \qquad 2\overline{)12}$$

6
12

2
4
6
8
10

12

2

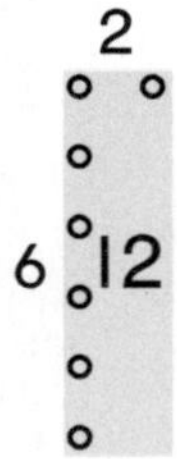

6 ° 12

## Card 2

$$5\overline{)10} \qquad 2\overline{)10}$$

5
10

2
4
6
8
10

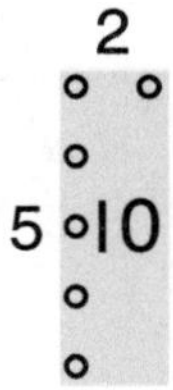

2

5 ° 10

## Card 3

$$4\overline{)8} \qquad 2\overline{)8}$$

4
8

2
4
6
8

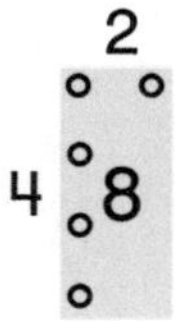

2

4 ° 8

## Card 4

$$3\overline{)6} \qquad 2\overline{)6}$$

3
6

2
4
6

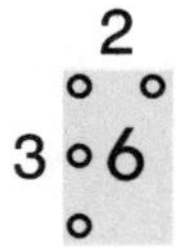

2

3 ° 6

## Card 5

$$3\overline{)9}$$

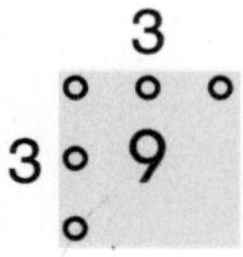

3
6
9

3

3 ° 9

## Card 6

$$9\overline{)18} \qquad 2\overline{)18}$$

9
18

2
4
6
8
10

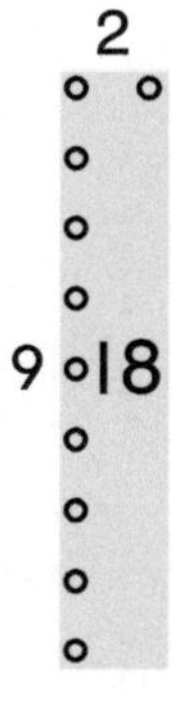

12
14
16
18

2

9 ° 18

## Card 7

$$8\overline{)16} \qquad 2\overline{)16}$$

8
16

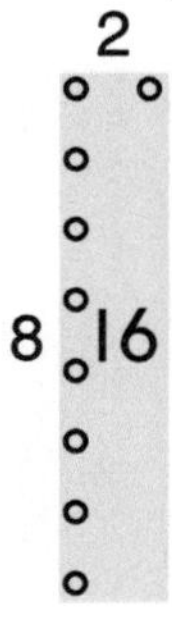

2
4
6
8
10

12
14
16

2

8 ° 16

## Card 8

$$7\overline{)14} \qquad 2\overline{)14}$$

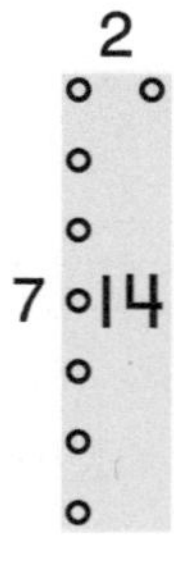

7
14

2
4
6
8
10

12
14

2

7 ° 14

$3\overline{)12}$

$12 \div 3$

$3\overline{)15}$

$15 \div 3$

$3\overline{)18}$

$18 \div 3$

$3\overline{)21}$

$21 \div 3$

$3\overline{)24}$

$24 \div 3$

$3\overline{)27}$

$27 \div 3$

$4\overline{)12}$

$12 \div 4$

$5\overline{)15}$

$15 \div 5$

| 7　　3 | 6　　3 | 5　　3 | 4　　3 |
|---|---|---|---|
| 3)21　7)21 | 3)18　6)18 | 3)15　5)15 | 3)12　4)12 |

Card 1:
3　　7
6　　14
9　　21
12
15

18
21

7
3 · 21

Card 2:
3　　6
6　　12
9　　18
12
15
18

6
3 · 18

Card 3:
3　　5
6　　10
9　　15
12
15

5
3 · 15

Card 4:
3　　4
6　　8
9　　12
12

4
3 · 12

| 3　　5 | 3　　4 | 9　　3 | 8　　3 |
|---|---|---|---|
| 5)15　3)15 | 4)12　3)12 | 3)27　9)27 | 3)24　8)24 |

Card 5:
5　　3
10　　6
15　　9
　　12
　　15

3
5 · 15

Card 6:
4　　3
8　　6
12　　9
　　12

3
4 · 12

Card 7:
3　　9
6　　18
9　　27
12
15

18
21
24
27

9
3 · 27

Card 8:
3　　8
6　　16
9　　24
12
15

18
21
24

8
3 · 24

Division Strategy Cards

| $6\overline{)18}$ | $7\overline{)21}$ | $8\overline{)24}$ | $9\overline{)27}$ |
|---|---|---|---|
| $18 \div 6$ | $21 \div 7$ | $24 \div 8$ | $27 \div 9$ |

| $4\overline{)16}$ | $4\overline{)20}$ | $4\overline{)24}$ | $4\overline{)28}$ |
|---|---|---|---|
| $16 \div 4$ | $20 \div 4$ | $24 \div 4$ | $28 \div 4$ |

**Row 1**

$$3 \qquad 9$$
$$9)\overline{27} \quad 3)\overline{27}$$

| | |
|---|---|
| 9 | 3 |
| 18 | 6 |
| 27 | 9 |
| | 12 |
| | 15 |
| | 18 |
| | 21 |
| | 24 |
| | 27 |

3
9 · 27

$$3 \qquad 8$$
$$8)\overline{24} \quad 3)\overline{24}$$

| | |
|---|---|
| 8 | 3 |
| 16 | 6 |
| 24 | 9 |
| | 12 |
| | 15 |
| | 18 |
| | 21 |
| | 24 |

3
8 · 24

$$3 \qquad 7$$
$$7)\overline{21} \quad 3)\overline{21}$$

| | |
|---|---|
| 7 | 3 |
| 14 | 6 |
| 21 | 9 |
| | 12 |
| | 15 |
| | 18 |
| | 21 |

3
7 · 21

$$3 \qquad 6$$
$$6)\overline{18} \quad 3)\overline{18}$$

| | |
|---|---|
| 6 | 3 |
| 12 | 6 |
| 18 | 9 |
| | 12 |
| | 15 |
| | 18 |

3
6 · 18

**Row 2**

$$7 \qquad 4$$
$$4)\overline{28} \quad 7)\overline{28}$$

| | |
|---|---|
| 4 | 7 |
| 8 | 14 |
| 12 | 21 |
| 16 | 28 |
| 20 | |
| 24 | |
| 28 | |

7
4 · 28

$$6 \qquad 4$$
$$4)\overline{24} \quad 6)\overline{24}$$

| | |
|---|---|
| 4 | 6 |
| 8 | 12 |
| 12 | 18 |
| 16 | 24 |
| 20 | |
| 24 | |

6
4 · 24

$$5 \qquad 4$$
$$4)\overline{20} \quad 5)\overline{20}$$

| | |
|---|---|
| 4 | 5 |
| 8 | 10 |
| 12 | 15 |
| 16 | 20 |
| 20 | |

5
4 · 20

$$4$$
$$4)\overline{16}$$

| |
|---|
| 4 |
| 8 |
| 12 |
| 16 |

4
4 · 16

Division Strategy Cards

| $4\overline{)32}$ | $4\overline{)36}$ | $5\overline{)20}$ | $6\overline{)24}$ |
|---|---|---|---|
| $32 \div 4$ | $36 \div 4$ | $20 \div 5$ | $24 \div 6$ |

| $7\overline{)28}$ | $8\overline{)32}$ | $9\overline{)36}$ | $5\overline{)25}$ |
|---|---|---|---|
| $28 \div 7$ | $32 \div 8$ | $36 \div 9$ | $25 \div 5$ |

$4$   $6$
$6\overline{)24}$   $4\overline{)24}$

| | |
|---|---|
| 6 | 4 |
| 12 | 8 |
| 18 | 12 |
| 24 | 16 |
| | 20 |
| | 24 |

4
6   24

---

$4$   $5$
$5\overline{)20}$   $4\overline{)20}$

| | |
|---|---|
| 5 | 4 |
| 10 | 8 |
| 15 | 12 |
| 20 | 16 |
| | 20 |

4
5   20

---

$9$   $4$
$4\overline{)36}$   $9\overline{)36}$

| | |
|---|---|
| 4 | 9 |
| 8 | 18 |
| 12 | 27 |
| 16 | 36 |
| 20 | |
| 24 | |
| 28 | |
| 32 | |
| 36 | |

9
4   36

---

$8$   $4$
$4\overline{)32}$   $8\overline{)32}$

| | |
|---|---|
| 4 | 8 |
| 8 | 16 |
| 12 | 24 |
| 16 | 32 |
| 20 | |
| 24 | |
| 28 | |
| 32 | |

8
4   32

---

$5$
$5\overline{)25}$

| |
|---|
| 5 |
| 10 |
| 15 |
| 20 |
| 25 |

5
5   25

---

$4$   $9$
$9\overline{)36}$   $4\overline{)36}$

| | |
|---|---|
| 9 | 4 |
| 18 | 8 |
| 27 | 12 |
| 36 | 16 |
| | 20 |
| | 24 |
| | 28 |
| | 32 |
| | 36 |

4
9   36

---

$4$   $8$
$8\overline{)32}$   $4\overline{)32}$

| | |
|---|---|
| 8 | 4 |
| 16 | 8 |
| 24 | 12 |
| 32 | 16 |
| | 20 |
| | 24 |
| | 28 |
| | 32 |

4
8   32

---

$4$   $7$
$7\overline{)28}$   $4\overline{)28}$

| | |
|---|---|
| 7 | 4 |
| 14 | 8 |
| 21 | 12 |
| 28 | 16 |
| | 20 |
| | 24 |
| | 28 |

4
7   28

Division Strategy Cards

| $5 \overline{)30}$ | $5 \overline{)35}$ | $5 \overline{)40}$ | $5 \overline{)45}$ |
|---|---|---|---|
| $30 \div 5$ | $35 \div 5$ | $40 \div 5$ | $45 \div 5$ |

| $6 \overline{)30}$ | $7 \overline{)35}$ | $8 \overline{)40}$ | $9 \overline{)45}$ |
|---|---|---|---|
| $30 \div 6$ | $35 \div 7$ | $40 \div 8$ | $45 \div 9$ |

# Division Strategy Cards

## Top Row

**Card 1**

$$9 \quad 5$$
$$5)\overline{45} \quad 9)\overline{45}$$

| 5 | 9 |
|---|---|
| 10 | 18 |
| 15 | 27 |
| 20 | 36 |
| 25 | 45 |
| 30 | |
| 35 | |
| 40 | |
| 45 | |

9 × 5 = 45

**Card 2**

$$8 \quad 5$$
$$5)\overline{40} \quad 8)\overline{40}$$

| 5 | 8 |
|---|---|
| 10 | 16 |
| 15 | 24 |
| 20 | 32 |
| 25 | 40 |
| 30 | |
| 35 | |
| 40 | |

8 × 5 = 40

**Card 3**

$$7 \quad 5$$
$$5)\overline{35} \quad 7)\overline{35}$$

| 5 | 7 |
|---|---|
| 10 | 14 |
| 15 | 21 |
| 20 | 28 |
| 25 | 35 |
| 30 | |
| 35 | |

7 × 5 = 35

**Card 4**

$$6 \quad 5$$
$$5)\overline{30} \quad 6)\overline{30}$$

| 5 | 6 |
|---|---|
| 10 | 12 |
| 15 | 18 |
| 20 | 24 |
| 25 | 30 |
| 30 | |

6 × 5 = 30

## Bottom Row

**Card 5**

$$5 \quad 9$$
$$9)\overline{45} \quad 5)\overline{45}$$

| 9 | 5 |
|---|---|
| 18 | 10 |
| 27 | 15 |
| 36 | 20 |
| 45 | 25 |
| | 30 |
| | 35 |
| | 40 |
| | 45 |

5 × 9 = 45

**Card 6**

$$5 \quad 8$$
$$8)\overline{40} \quad 5)\overline{40}$$

| 8 | 5 |
|---|---|
| 16 | 10 |
| 24 | 15 |
| 32 | 20 |
| 40 | 25 |
| | 30 |
| | 35 |
| | 40 |

5 × 8 = 40

**Card 7**

$$5 \quad 7$$
$$7)\overline{35} \quad 5)\overline{35}$$

| 7 | 5 |
|---|---|
| 14 | 10 |
| 21 | 15 |
| 28 | 20 |
| 35 | 25 |
| | 30 |
| | 35 |

5 × 7 = 35

**Card 8**

$$5 \quad 6$$
$$6)\overline{30} \quad 5)\overline{30}$$

| 6 | 5 |
|---|---|
| 12 | 10 |
| 18 | 15 |
| 24 | 20 |
| 30 | 25 |
| | 30 |

5 × 6 = 30

Division Strategy Cards

$6 \overline{)36}$

$36 \div 6$

$6 \overline{)42}$

$42 \div 6$

$6 \overline{)48}$

$48 \div 6$

$6 \overline{)54}$

$54 \div 6$

$7 \overline{)42}$

$42 \div 7$

$8 \overline{)48}$

$48 \div 8$

$9 \overline{)54}$

$54 \div 9$

$7 \overline{)49}$

$49 \div 7$

$9 \quad 6$

$6\overline{)54} \quad 9\overline{)54}$

| | |
|---|---|
| 6 | 9 |
| 12 | 18 |
| 18 | 27 |
| 24 | 36 |
| 30 | 45 |
| | |
| 36 | 54 |
| 42 | |
| 48 | |
| 54 | |

9

6 — 54

$8 \quad 6$

$6\overline{)48} \quad 8\overline{)48}$

| | |
|---|---|
| 6 | 8 |
| 12 | 16 |
| 18 | 24 |
| 24 | 32 |
| 30 | 40 |
| | |
| 36 | 48 |
| 42 | |
| 48 | |

8

6 — 48

$7 \quad 6$

$6\overline{)42} \quad 7\overline{)42}$

| | |
|---|---|
| 6 | 7 |
| 12 | 14 |
| 18 | 21 |
| 24 | 28 |
| 30 | 35 |
| | |
| 36 | 42 |
| 42 | |

7

6 — 42

$6$

$6\overline{)36}$

| |
|---|
| 6 |
| 12 |
| 18 |
| 24 |
| 30 |
| |
| 36 |

6

6 — 36

$7$

$7\overline{)49}$

| |
|---|
| 7 |
| 14 |
| 21 |
| 28 |
| 35 |
| |
| 42 |
| 49 |

7

7 — 49

$6 \quad 9$

$9\overline{)54} \quad 6\overline{)54}$

| | |
|---|---|
| 9 | 6 |
| 18 | 12 |
| 27 | 18 |
| 36 | 24 |
| 45 | 30 |
| | |
| 54 | 36 |
| | 42 |
| | 48 |
| | 54 |

6

9 — 54

$6 \quad 8$

$8\overline{)48} \quad 6\overline{)48}$

| | |
|---|---|
| 8 | 6 |
| 16 | 12 |
| 24 | 18 |
| 32 | 24 |
| 40 | 30 |
| | |
| 48 | 36 |
| | 42 |
| | 48 |

6

8 — 48

$6 \quad 7$

$7\overline{)42} \quad 6\overline{)42}$

| | |
|---|---|
| 7 | 6 |
| 14 | 12 |
| 21 | 18 |
| 28 | 24 |
| 35 | 30 |
| | |
| 42 | 36 |
| | 42 |

6

7 — 42

Division Strategy Cards

| $7 \overline{)56}$ | $7 \overline{)63}$ | $8 \overline{)56}$ | $9 \overline{)63}$ |
|---|---|---|---|
| $56 \div 7$ | $63 \div 7$ | $56 \div 8$ | $63 \div 9$ |

| $8 \overline{)64}$ | $8 \overline{)72}$ | $9 \overline{)72}$ | $9 \overline{)81}$ |
|---|---|---|---|
| $64 \div 8$ | $72 \div 8$ | $72 \div 9$ | $81 \div 9$ |

## Card 1

$9\overline{)63}$  $7\overline{)63}$

| 9 | 7 |
|---|---|
| 18 | 14 |
| 27 | 21 |
| 36 | 28 |
| 45 | 35 |
| 54 | 42 |
| 63 | 49 |
|  | 56 |
|  | 63 |

7

9  63

## Card 2

$8\overline{)56}$  $7\overline{)56}$

| 8 | 7 |
|---|---|
| 16 | 14 |
| 24 | 21 |
| 32 | 28 |
| 40 | 35 |
| 48 | 42 |
| 56 | 49 |
|  | 56 |

7

8  56

## Card 3

$7\overline{)63}$  $9\overline{)63}$

| 7 | 9 |
|---|---|
| 14 | 18 |
| 21 | 27 |
| 28 | 36 |
| 35 | 45 |
| 42 | 54 |
| 49 | 63 |
| 56 |  |
| 63 |  |

9

7  63

## Card 4

$7\overline{)56}$  $8\overline{)56}$

| 7 | 8 |
|---|---|
| 14 | 16 |
| 21 | 24 |
| 28 | 32 |
| 35 | 40 |
| 42 | 48 |
| 49 | 56 |
| 56 |  |

8

7  56

## Card 5

$9\overline{)81}$

| 9 |
|---|
| 18 |
| 27 |
| 36 |
| 45 |
| 54 |
| 63 |
| 72 |
| 81 |

9

9  81

## Card 6

$9\overline{)72}$  $8\overline{)72}$

| 9 | 8 |
|---|---|
| 18 | 16 |
| 27 | 24 |
| 36 | 32 |
| 45 | 40 |
| 54 | 48 |
| 63 | 56 |
| 72 | 64 |
|  | 72 |

8

9  72

## Card 7

$8\overline{)72}$  $9\overline{)72}$

| 8 | 9 |
|---|---|
| 16 | 18 |
| 24 | 27 |
| 32 | 36 |
| 40 | 45 |
| 48 | 54 |
| 56 | 63 |
| 64 | 72 |
| 72 |  |

9

8  72

## Card 8

$8\overline{)64}$

| 8 |
|---|
| 16 |
| 24 |
| 32 |
| 40 |
| 48 |
| 56 |
| 64 |

8

8  64

Division Strategy Cards

► ⦿ PATH to FLUENCY **Find the Area**

The area of a rectangle is the number of square units that fit inside of it.

**Write a multiplication equation to represent the area of each rectangle. Then shade a whole number of rows in each rectangle and write a multiplication and addition equation to represent the area of each rectangle.**

**1.**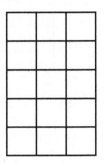

**2.**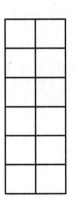

**3.**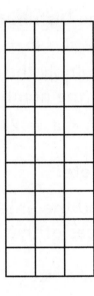

_____   _____   _____

_____   _____   _____

_____   _____   _____

**Make a rectangle drawing to represent each problem. Then give the product.**

**4.** $5 \times 3 =$ _____

**5.** $7 * 2 =$ _____

**6.** $2 \bullet 9 =$ _____

VOCABULARY
Distributive Property

► PATH to FLUENCY **Different Ways to Find Area**

The large rectangle has been divided into two small rectangles.
You can find the area of the large rectangle in two ways:

- Add the areas of the two small rectangles:

  $5 \times 3 = \quad$ 15 square units

  $2 \times 3 = \quad \underline{\quad 6 \text{ square units}}$

  21 square units

  The **Distributive Property** is shown by

  $7 \times 3 = (5 + 2) \times 3 = (5 \times 3) + (2 \times 3)$

- Multiply the number of rows in the large rectangle by the number of square units in each row:

  $7 \times 3 = 21$ square units

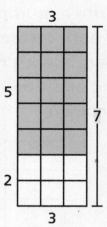

**Complete.**

7. Find the area of the large rectangle by finding the areas of the two small rectangles and adding them.

   _____

   _____

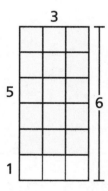

8. Find the area of the large rectangle by multiplying the number of rows by the number of square units in each row.

   _____

   _____

9. Find this product: $5 \times 4 = $ _____

10. Find this product: $2 \times 4 = $ _____

11. Use your answers to Exercises 9 and 10 to find this product: $7 \times 4 = $ _____

Multiplication and Area

## ► Make Sense of Problems

**Write an equation and solve the problem.**

*Show your work.*

1. The garden shop received a shipment of 12 rose bushes. They arranged the rose bushes in 3 rows with the same number of bushes in each row. How many rose bushes were in each row?

   _____

2. Eric saw 4 stop signs on the way to school. Each stop sign had 8 sides. How many sides were on all 4 stop signs?

   _____

3. Ed needs 14 batteries. If he buys the batteries in packages of 2, how many packages of batteries will he need to buy?

   _____

4. A flag has 5 rows of stars with the same number of stars in each row. There are 35 stars on the flag. How many stars are in each row?

   _____

5. Melia learned in science class that insects have 6 legs. What is the total number of legs on 9 insects?

   _____

6. Stan has 4 model car kits. Each kit comes with 5 tires. How many tires does Stan have altogether?

   _____

## ▶ Make Sense of Problems (continued)

**Write an equation and solve the problem.**

*Show your work.*

7. Maria bought a shoe rack. The shoe rack has 3 rows with places for 6 shoes on each row. How many shoes can be placed on the shoe rack?

   _____

8. The park has 4 swing sets with the same number of swings on each set. There is a total of 16 swings at the park. How many swings are on each swing set?

   _____

9. Amanda has 27 seashells in her collection. She displayed the seashells in 3 rows with the same number of seashells in each row. How many seashells are in each row?

   _____

10. The art room has 4 round tables. There are 6 chairs around each table. Altogether, how many chairs are around the tables?

    _____

11. Shanna is making bead necklaces for the craft fair. She can make 3 necklaces a day. She plans to make 21 necklaces. How many days will it take her to make the necklaces?

    _____

12. One section on a plane has 9 rows of seats. Five passengers can sit in each row. How many passengers could sit in this section of the plane?

    _____

► PATH to FLUENCY **Play *Solve the Stack***

**Read the rules for playing *Solve the Stack*. Then play the game with your group.**

> **Rules for *Solve the Stack***
>
> *Number of players:* 2–4
>
> *What you will need:* 1 set of multiplication and division Strategy Cards
>
> 1. Shuffle the cards. Place them exercise side up in the center of the table.
>
> 2. Players take turns. On each turn, a player finds the answer to the multiplication or division on the top card and then turns the card over to check the answer.
>
> 3. If a player's answer is correct, he or she takes the card. If it is incorrect, the card is placed at the bottom of the stack.
>
> 4. Play ends when there are no more cards in the stack. The player with the most cards wins.

► (PATH to FLUENCY) **Play *High Card Wins***

**Read the rules for playing *High Card Wins*. Then play the game with your partner.**

---

**Rules for *High Card Wins***

*Number of players:* 2

*What you will need:* 1 set of multiplication and division Strategy Cards for 2s, 3s, 4s, 5s, 9s

1. Shuffle the cards. Deal all the cards evenly between the two players.

2. Players put their stacks in front of them, exercise side up.

3. Each player takes the top card from his or her stack and puts it exercise side up in the center of the table.

4. Each player says the multiplication or division answer and then turns the card over to check. Then players do one of the following:

   • If one player says the wrong answer, the other player takes both cards and puts them at the bottom of his or her pile.

   • If both players say the wrong answer, both players take back their cards and put them at the bottom of their piles.

   • If both players say the correct answer, the player with the higher product or quotient takes both cards and puts them at the bottom of his or her pile. If the products or quotients are the same, the players set the cards aside and play another round. The winner of the next round takes all the cards.

5. Play continues until one player has all the cards.

---

© Houghton Mifflin Harcourt Publishing Company

► **PATH to FLUENCY** **Review Strategies**

**Complete.**

1. Emily knows that $4 \times 10 = 40$. How can she use subtraction and multiples of 9 to find $4 \times 9$?

_____

2. Joey knows the multiplications $5 \times 4$ and $4 \times 4$. How can he use their products to find $9 \times 4$?

_____

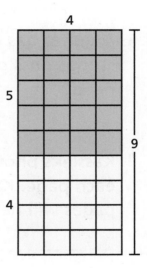

3. Hannah knows that each division has a related multiplication. What related multiplication fact can she use to find $18 \div 3$?

_____

4. Kyle knows that $5 \times 3 = 15$. How can he use the 5s shortcut to find $8 \times 3$?

_____

5. Letitia knows that $5 \times 4 = 20$. How can she use the 5s shortcut to find $9 \times 4$?

_____

6. Jorge knows that $6 \times 9 = 54$. How can he use the Commutative Property or arrays to find $9 \times 6$?

_____

_____

▶ **Make Sense of Problems**

**Write an equation and solve the problem.**

*Show your work.*

7. Jordan has 32 peaches. He wants to divide them equally among 4 baskets. How many peaches will he put in each basket?

_____

8. A guitar has 6 strings. If Taylor replaces all the strings on 3 guitars, how many strings does he need?

_____

9. Kassler's photograph album holds 5 pictures on each page. Kassler has 40 pictures. How many pages will he fill?

_____

10. Emily rides her bike 3 miles every day. How many miles does she ride her bike in a week?

_____

11. Ruel has a board 36 inches long. He wants to saw it into equal pieces 9 inches long. How many pieces will he get?

_____

▶ **Write a Word Problem**

12. Write a word problem that can be solved using the equation $7 \times 10 = 70$.

_____

_____

## ► Explore Patterns with 1s

### What patterns do you see below?

1.

$1 = 1 \times \boxed{1} = 1$

$2 = 2 \times \boxed{1} = 1 + 1$

$3 = 3 \times \boxed{1} = 1 + 1 + 1$

$4 = 4 \times \boxed{1} = 1 + 1 + 1 + 1$

$5 = 5 \times \boxed{1} = 1 + 1 + 1 + 1 + 1$

$6 = 6 \times \boxed{1} = 1 + 1 + 1 + 1 + 1 + 1$

$7 = 7 \times \boxed{1} = 1 + 1 + 1 + 1 + 1 + 1 + 1$

$8 = 8 \times \boxed{1} = 1 + 1 + 1 + 1 + 1 + 1 + 1 + 1$

$9 = 9 \times \boxed{1} = 1 + 1 + 1 + 1 + 1 + 1 + 1 + 1 + 1$

$10 = 10 \times \boxed{1} = 1 + 1 + 1 + 1 + 1 + 1 + 1 + 1 + 1 + 1$

## ► Explore Patterns with 0s

### What patterns do you see below?

2.

$1 \times \boxed{0} = 0$

$2 \times \boxed{0} = 0 + 0$

$3 \times \boxed{0} = 0 + 0 + 0$

$4 \times \boxed{0} = 0 + 0 + 0 + 0$

$5 \times \boxed{0} = 0 + 0 + 0 + 0 + 0$

$6 \times \boxed{0} = 0 + 0 + 0 + 0 + 0 + 0$

$7 \times \boxed{0} = 0 + 0 + 0 + 0 + 0 + 0 + 0$

$8 \times \boxed{0} = 0 + 0 + 0 + 0 + 0 + 0 + 0 + 0$

$9 \times \boxed{0} = 0 + 0 + 0 + 0 + 0 + 0 + 0 + 0 + 0$

$10 \times \boxed{0} = 0 + 0 + 0 + 0 + 0 + 0 + 0 + 0 + 0 + 0$

► **PATH to FLUENCY** **Multiplication Properties and Division Rules**

### Properties and Rules

| Property for 1 | Division Rule for 1 | Zero Property | Division Rule for 0 |
|---|---|---|---|
| $1 \times 6 = 6$ <br> $6 \times 1 = 6$ | $8 \div 1 = 8$ <br> $8 \div 8 = 1$ | $6 \times 0 = 0$ <br> $0 \times 6 = 0$ | $0 \div 6 = 0$ <br> $6 \div 0$ is impossible. |

### Associative Property of Multiplication

When you group factors in different ways, the product stays the same. The parentheses tell you which numbers to multiply first.

$(3 \times 2) \times 5 = \boxed{\phantom{00}}$    $3 \times (2 \times 5) = \boxed{\phantom{00}}$

$6 \quad \times 5 = 30$    $3 \times \quad 10 \quad = 30$

**Find each product.**

3. $2 \times (6 \times 1) = \boxed{\phantom{0}}$    4. $(4 \times 2) \times 2 = \boxed{\phantom{0}}$    5. $7 \times (1 \times 5) = \boxed{\phantom{0}}$

6. $(9 \times 8) \times 0 = \boxed{\phantom{0}}$    7. $3 \times (2 \times 3) = \boxed{\phantom{0}}$    8. $6 \times (0 \times 7) = \boxed{\phantom{0}}$

**Solve each problem.**

*Show your work.*

9. Shawn gave 1 nickel to each of his sisters. If he gave away 3 nickels, how many sisters does Shawn have? _____

10. Kara has 3 boxes. She put 0 toys in each box. How many toys are in the boxes? _____

11. There are 3 tables in the library. Each table has 2 piles of books on it. If there are 3 books in each pile, how many books are on the tables?

_____

► PATH to FLUENCY **Identify Addition and Multiplication Properties**

| Addition Properties | Multiplication Properties |
|---|---|
| **A. Commutative Property of Addition** The order in which numbers are added does not change their sum.<br>$3 + 5 = 5 + 3$ | **D. Commutative Property of Multiplication** The order in which numbers are multiplied does not change their product.<br>$3 \times 5 = 5 \times 3$ |
| **B. Associative Property of Addition** The way in which numbers are grouped does not change their sum.<br>$(3 + 2) + 5 = 3 + (2 + 5)$ | **E. Associative Property of Multiplication** The way in which numbers are grouped does not change their product.<br>$(3 \times 2) \times 5 = 3 \times (2 \times 5)$ |
| **C. Identity Property of Addition** If 0 is added to a number, the sum equals that number.<br>$3 + 0 = 3$ | **F. Identity Property of Multiplication** The product of 1 and any number is that number.<br>$3 \times 1 = 3$ |
| | **G. Zero Property of Multiplication** If 0 is multiplied by a number, the product is 0.<br>$3 \times 0 = 0$ |

**Write the letter of the property that is shown.**

**12.** $1 \times 9 = 9$ _____

**13.** $5 + (6 + 7) = (5 + 6) + 7$ _____

**14.** $5 \times 0 = 0$ _____

**15.** $8 + 0 = 8$ _____

**16.** $3 \times 9 = \boxed{\phantom{0}} \times 3$ _____

**17.** $(2 \times 1) \times 3 = 2 \times (\boxed{\phantom{0}} \times 3)$ _____

1-15
**Class Activity**

**Name**

**Date**

PATH to
FLUENCY

# ▶ Use Properties to Solve Equations

**Use properties and rules to find the unknown numbers.**

18. $5 \times 8 = \boxed{\phantom{0}} \times 5$    19. $4 + 3 = \boxed{\phantom{0}} + 4$    20. $0 \div 8 = \boxed{\phantom{0}}$

21. $4 \div 4 = \boxed{\phantom{0}}$    22. $(3 \times 2) \times 4 = 3 \times (\boxed{\phantom{0}} \times 4)$    23. $6 \times 2 = 2 \times \boxed{\phantom{0}}$

24. $5 \times 3 = \boxed{\phantom{0}} \times 5$    25. $(6 + 2) + 2 = 6 + (\boxed{\phantom{0}} + 2)$    26. $11 + 0 = \boxed{\phantom{0}}$

27. $65 \times 1 = \boxed{\phantom{0}}$    28. $5 \times (2 \times 6) = (5 \times 2) \times \boxed{\phantom{0}}$    29. $17 \times 0 = \boxed{\phantom{0}}$

# ▶ Use Equations to Demonstrate Properties

**Write your own equation that shows the property.**

30. Commutative Property of
Multiplication

_____

31. Associative Property of
Addition

_____

32. Identity Property of
Addition

_____

33. Identity Property of
Multiplication

_____

34. Associative Property of
Multiplication

_____

35. Zero Property of
Multiplication

_____

36. Commutative Property of
Addition

_____

Multiply and Divide with 1 and 0

► **Identify Types of Problems**

**Read each problem and decide what type of problem it is. Write the letter from the list below. Then write an equation to solve the problem.**

a. Array Multiplication

b. Array Division

c. Equal Groups Multiplication

d. Equal Groups Division with an Unknown Group Size

e. Equal Groups Division with an Unknown Multiplier (number of groups)

f. None of the above

1. Mrs. Ostrega has 3 children. She wants to buy 5 juice boxes for each child. How many juice boxes does she need?

2. Sophie picked 15 peaches from one tree and 3 peaches from another. How many peaches did she pick in all?

3. Zamir brought 21 treats to the dog park. He divided the treats equally among the 7 dogs that were there. How many treats did each dog get?

4. Art said he could make 12 muffins in his muffin pan. The pan has space for 3 muffins in a row. How many rows does the muffin pan have?

5. Bia is helping with the lights for the school play. Each box of light bulbs has 6 rows, with 3 bulbs in each row. How many light bulbs are in each box?

6. Tryouts were held to find triplets to act in a commercial for Triple-Crunch Cereal. If 24 children tried out for the commercial, how many sets of triplets tried out?

## ► Make Sense of Problems

**Write an equation and solve the problem.**

*Show your work.*

7. The produce market sells oranges in bags of 6. Santos bought 1 bag. How many oranges did he buy?

_____

8. Janine bought a jewelry organizer with 36 pockets. The pockets are arranged in 9 rows with the same number of pockets in each row. How many pockets are in each row?

_____

9. A parking lot has 9 rows of parking spaces. Each row has 7 spaces. How many cars can park in the lot?

_____

10. Keshawn bought 18 animal stickers for his sisters. He gave 6 stickers to each sister and had none left. How many sisters does Keshawn have?

_____

11. The pet store put 3 fish bowls on a shelf. The store put 0 goldfish in each bowl. How many goldfish are in the bowls?

_____

## ► Write a Word Problem

12. Write a word problem that can be solved using $0 \div 5$, where 5 is the group size.

_____

_____

_____

▶ PATH to FLUENCY **Play** *Multiplication Three-in-a-Row*

**Read the rules for playing *Multiplication Three-in-a-Row*.**
**Then play the game with a partner.**

---

**Rules for *Multiplication Three-in-a-Row***

*Number of players:* 2

*What You Will Need:* A set of multiplication Strategy
Cards, *Three-in-a-Row* Game Grids for each player
(see page 75)

1. Each player looks through the cards and writes
   any nine of the products in the squares of a Game
   Grid. A player may write the same product more
   than once.

2. Shuffle the cards and place them exercise side up
   in the center of the table.

3. Players take turns. On each turn, a player finds the
   answer to the multiplication on the top card and
   then turns the card over to check the answer.

4. If the answer is correct, the player looks to see if
   the product is on the game grid. If it is, the player
   puts an X through that grid square. If the answer
   is wrong, or if the product is not on the grid, the
   player does not mark anything. The player then
   puts the card problem side up on the bottom of
   the stack.

5. The first player to mark three squares in a row
   (horizontally, vertically, or diagonally) wins.

---

**Name** _____  **Date** _____

▶ (PATH to FLUENCY) Play *Division Race*

**Read the rules for playing *Division Race*. Then play the game with a partner.**

---

**Rules for *Division Race***

*Number of players:* 2

*What You Will Need:* a set of division Strategy Cards, the *Division Race* game board (see page 76), a different game piece for each player

1. Shuffle the cards and then place them exercise side up on the table.

2. Both players put their game pieces on "START."

3. Players take turns. On each turn, a player finds the answer to the division on the top card and then turns the card over to check the answer.

4. If the answer is correct, the player moves *forward* that number of spaces. If a player's answer is wrong, the player moves *back* a number of spaces equal to the correct answer. Players cannot move back beyond the "START" square. The player puts the card on the bottom of the stack.

5. If a player lands on a space with special instructions, he or she should follow those instructions.

6. The game ends when everyone lands on or passes the "End" square.

---

Start

End

**Slide back!**

Skip a turn.

Move your partner ahead 2 spaces.

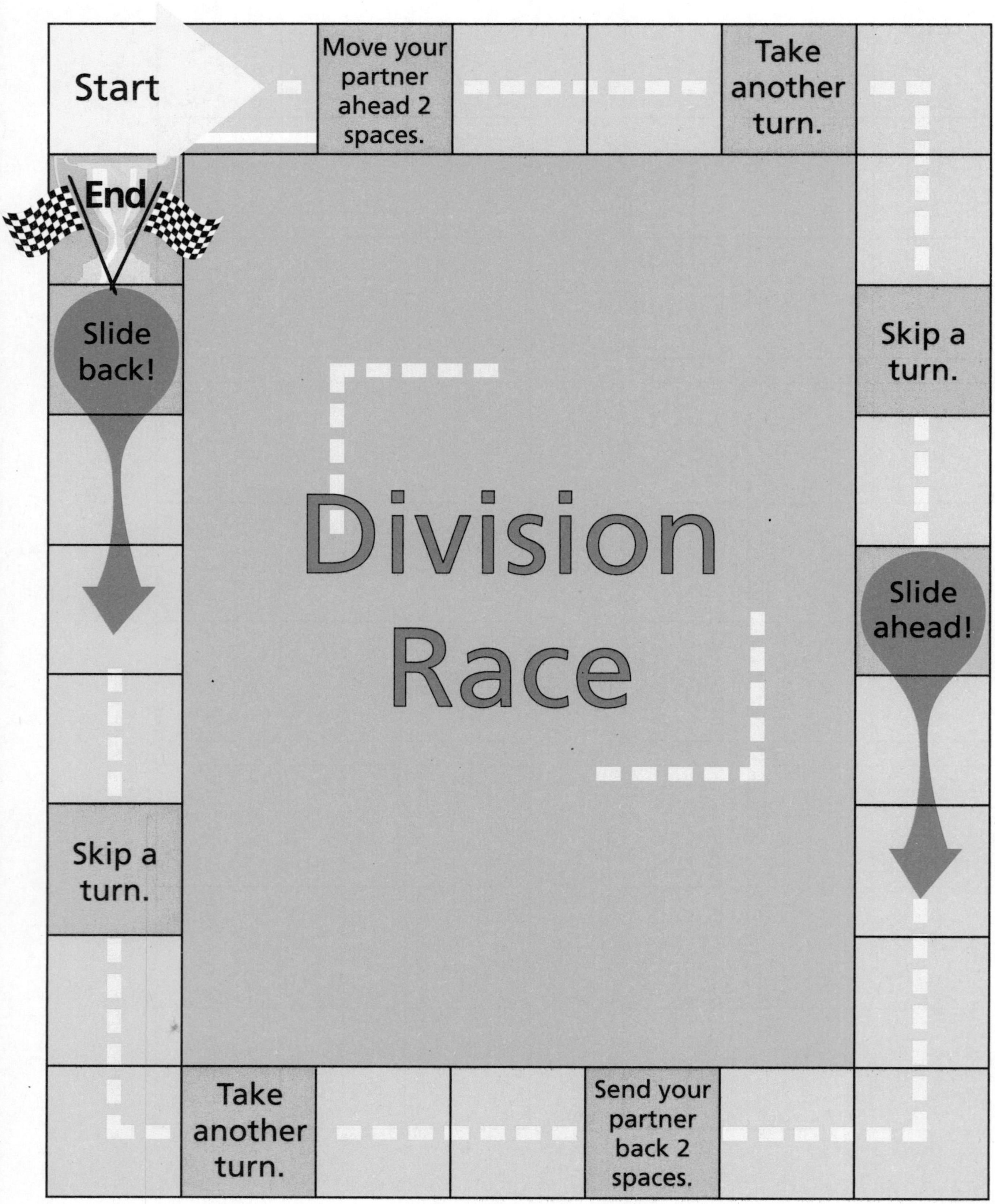

Take another turn.

Skip a turn.

# Division Race

Slide ahead!

Take another turn.

Send your partner back 2 spaces.

*Division Race* Game Board

**Name**

**Date**

► PATH to FLUENCY **Dashes 9–12**

## Complete each Dash. Check your answers on page 82.

| Dash 9 2s, 5s, 9s, 10s Multiplications | Dash 10 2s, 5s, 9s, 10s Divisions | Dash 11 3s, 4s, 0s, 1s Multiplications | Dash 12 3s, 4s, 1s Divisions |
|---|---|---|---|
| a. $4 \times 5 =$ _____ | a. $8 / 2 =$ _____ | a. $3 \times 0 =$ _____ | a. $12 / 4 =$ _____ |
| b. $10 \cdot 3 =$ _____ | b. $50 \div 10 =$ _____ | b. $4 \cdot 6 =$ _____ | b. $5 \div 1 =$ _____ |
| c. $8 * 9 =$ _____ | c. $15 / 5 =$ _____ | c. $9 * 1 =$ _____ | c. $21 / 3 =$ _____ |
| d. $6 \times 2 =$ _____ | d. $63 \div 9 =$ _____ | d. $3 \times 3 =$ _____ | d. $1 \div 1 =$ _____ |
| e. $5 \cdot 7 =$ _____ | e. $90 / 10 =$ _____ | e. $8 \cdot 4 =$ _____ | e. $16 / 4 =$ _____ |
| f. $10 * 5 =$ _____ | f. $90 \div 9 =$ _____ | f. $0 * 5 =$ _____ | f. $9 \div 3 =$ _____ |
| g. $8 \times 2 =$ _____ | g. $35 / 5 =$ _____ | g. $1 \times 6 =$ _____ | g. $32 / 4 =$ _____ |
| h. $6 \cdot 10 =$ _____ | h. $14 \div 2 =$ _____ | h. $4 \cdot 3 =$ _____ | h. $8 \div 1 =$ _____ |
| i. $9 * 3 =$ _____ | i. $27 / 9 =$ _____ | i. $7 * 4 =$ _____ | i. $24 / 4 =$ _____ |
| j. $2 \times 9 =$ _____ | j. $45 / 5 =$ _____ | j. $3 \times 7 =$ _____ | j. $18 / 3 =$ _____ |
| k. $5 \cdot 8 =$ _____ | k. $10 \div 10 =$ _____ | k. $0 \cdot 1 =$ _____ | k. $10 \div 1 =$ _____ |
| l. $10 * 7 =$ _____ | l. $25 / 5 =$ _____ | l. $10 * 1 =$ _____ | l. $40 / 4 =$ _____ |
| m. $5 \times 5 =$ _____ | m. $54 \div 9 =$ _____ | m. $4 \times 4 =$ _____ | m. $12 \div 3 =$ _____ |
| n. $1 \cdot 5 =$ _____ | n. $6 / 2 =$ _____ | n. $9 \cdot 3 =$ _____ | n. $6 / 3 =$ _____ |
| o. $9 * 6 =$ _____ | o. $72 \div 9 =$ _____ | o. $8 * 0 =$ _____ | o. $4 \div 4 =$ _____ |
| p. $10 \times 10 =$ _____ | p. $40 / 5 =$ _____ | p. $5 \times 4 =$ _____ | p. $7 / 1 =$ _____ |
| q. $4 \cdot 2 =$ _____ | q. $80 \div 10 =$ _____ | q. $1 \cdot 6 =$ _____ | q. $28 \div 4 =$ _____ |
| r. $10 * 8 =$ _____ | r. $18 \div 2 =$ _____ | r. $3 * 8 =$ _____ | r. $24 \div 3 =$ _____ |
| s. $3 \times 9 =$ _____ | s. $36 / 9 =$ _____ | s. $4 \times 9 =$ _____ | s. $20 / 4 =$ _____ |
| t. $9 \cdot 9 =$ _____ | t. $30 \div 5 =$ _____ | t. $0 \cdot 4 =$ _____ | t. $27 \div 3 =$ _____ |

► PATH to FLUENCY **Dashes 9A–12A**

## Complete each Dash. Check your answers on page 82.

| Dash 9A<br>2s, 5s, 9s, 10s<br>Multiplications | Dash 10A<br>2s, 5s, 9s, 10s<br>Divisions | Dash 11A<br>3s, 4s, 0s, 1s<br>Multiplications | Dash 12A<br>3s, 4s, 1s<br>Divisions |
|---|---|---|---|
| a. $9 \times 9 =$ _____ | a. $30 / 5 =$ _____ | a. $0 \times 4 =$ _____ | a. $10 / 1 =$ _____ |
| b. $4 * 5 =$ _____ | b. $18 \div 2 =$ _____ | b. $4 * 9 =$ _____ | b. $40 \div 4 =$ _____ |
| c. $10 \cdot 3 =$ _____ | c. $40 / 5 =$ _____ | c. $3 \cdot 8 =$ _____ | c. $12 / 3 =$ _____ |
| d. $3 \times 9 =$ _____ | d. $6 \div 2 =$ _____ | d. $3 \times 0 =$ _____ | d. $6 \div 3 =$ _____ |
| e. $10 * 8 =$ _____ | e. $25 / 5 =$ _____ | e. $4 * 6 =$ _____ | e. $4 / 4 =$ _____ |
| f. $6 \cdot 2 =$ _____ | f. $45 \div 5 =$ _____ | f. $9 \cdot 1 =$ _____ | f. $7 \div 1 =$ _____ |
| g. $8 \times 9 =$ _____ | g. $14 / 2 =$ _____ | g. $3 \times 3 =$ _____ | g. $28 / 4 =$ _____ |
| h. $4 * 2 =$ _____ | h. $90 \div 9 =$ _____ | h. $8 * 4 =$ _____ | h. $24 \div 3 =$ _____ |
| i. $10 \cdot 10 =$ _____ | i. $63 / 9 =$ _____ | i. $0 \cdot 5 =$ _____ | i. $20 / 4 =$ _____ |
| j. $9 \times 6 =$ _____ | j. $50 \div 10 =$ _____ | j. $1 \times 6 =$ _____ | j. $27 \div 3 =$ _____ |
| k. $5 * 7 =$ _____ | k. $8 / 2 =$ _____ | k. $5 * 4 =$ _____ | k. $12 / 4 =$ _____ |
| l. $10 \cdot 5 =$ _____ | l. $15 \div 5 =$ _____ | l. $8 \cdot 0 =$ _____ | l. $5 \div 1 =$ _____ |
| m. $8 \times 2 =$ _____ | m. $90 / 10 =$ _____ | m. $9 \times 3 =$ _____ | m. $21 / 3 =$ _____ |
| n. $6 * 10 =$ _____ | n. $35 \div 5 =$ _____ | n. $4 * 4 =$ _____ | n. $1 \div 1 =$ _____ |
| o. $2 * 9 =$ _____ | o. $27 / 9 =$ _____ | o. $10 \cdot 1 =$ _____ | o. $16 / 4 =$ _____ |
| p. $9 \cdot 6 =$ _____ | p. $10 \div 10 =$ _____ | p. $4 \times 3 =$ _____ | p. $9 \div 3 =$ _____ |
| q. $1 \times 5 =$ _____ | q. $54 / 9 =$ _____ | q. $7 * 4 =$ _____ | q. $32 / 4 =$ _____ |
| r. $5 * 5 =$ _____ | r. $72 \div 9 =$ _____ | r. $3 \cdot 7 =$ _____ | r. $8 \div 1 =$ _____ |
| s. $10 \cdot 7 =$ _____ | s. $80 / 10 =$ _____ | s. $0 \times 1 =$ _____ | s. $24 / 4 =$ _____ |
| t. $5 \times 8 =$ _____ | t. $36 \div 9 =$ _____ | t. $10 * 1 =$ _____ | t. $18 \div 3 =$ _____ |

## ► Answers to Dashes 1–8

Use this sheet to check your answers to the Dashes on pages 77 and 78.

| Dash 1<br>2s and<br>5s<br>× | Dash 2<br>2s and<br>5s<br>÷ | Dash 3<br>9s and<br>10s<br>× | Dash 4<br>9s and<br>10s<br>÷ | Dash 5<br>3s and<br>4s<br>× | Dash 6<br>3s and<br>4s<br>÷ | Dash 7<br>0s and<br>1s<br>× | Dash 8<br>1s and<br>$n \div n$<br>÷ |
|---|---|---|---|---|---|---|---|
| a. 12 | a. 9 | a. 90 | a. 10 | a. 27 | a. 3 | a. 0 | a. 1 |
| b. 45 | b. 5 | b. 30 | b. 1 | b. 8 | b. 5 | b. 4 | b. 8 |
| c. 14 | c. 4 | c. 9 | c. 3 | c. 18 | c. 7 | c. 0 | c. 1 |
| d. 40 | d. 9 | d. 20 | d. 9 | d. 40 | d. 4 | d. 8 | d. 6 |
| e. 8 | e. 8 | e. 81 | e. 7 | e. 3 | e. 3 | e. 0 | e. 1 |
| f. 15 | f. 4 | f. 60 | f. 5 | f. 4 | f. 8 | f. 3 | f. 4 |
| g. 2 | g. 2 | g. 36 | g. 1 | g. 30 | g. 6 | g. 0 | g. 1 |
| h. 35 | h. 8 | h. 100 | h. 6 | h. 20 | h. 6 | h. 2 | h. 2 |
| i. 18 | i. 10 | i. 18 | i. 5 | i. 9 | i. 10 | i. 0 | i. 1 |
| j. 20 | j. 7 | j. 10 | j. 3 | j. 16 | j. 4 | j. 10 | j. 9 |
| k. 10 | k. 3 | k. 63 | k. 2 | k. 24 | k. 2 | k. 0 | k. 1 |
| l. 5 | l. 3 | l. 50 | l. 8 | l. 28 | l. 7 | l. 1 | l. 5 |
| m. 4 | m. 7 | m. 72 | m. 4 | m. 6 | m. 8 | m. 0 | m. 1 |
| n. 50 | n. 1 | n. 70 | n. 2 | n. 36 | n. 5 | n. 5 | n. 1 |
| o. 20 | o. 5 | o. 27 | o. 6 | o. 21 | o. 9 | o. 0 | o. 7 |
| p. 30 | p. 2 | p. 40 | p. 10 | p. 12 | p. 5 | p. 6 | p. 1 |
| q. 6 | q. 3 | q. 45 | q. 9 | q. 15 | q. 9 | q. 0 | q. 10 |
| r. 25 | r. 6 | r. 80 | r. 7 | r. 24 | r. 9 | r. 0 | r. 1 |
| s. 16 | s. 1 | s. 54 | s. 8 | s. 12 | s. 2 | s. 7 | s. 3 |
| t. 30 | t. 9 | t. 90 | t. 4 | t. 32 | t. 10 | t. 9 | t. 0 |

# ► Answers to Dashes 9–12, 9A–12A

## Use this sheet to check your answers to the Dashes on pages 79 and 80.

| Dash 9 × | Dash 10 ÷ | Dash 11 × | Dash 12 ÷ | Dash 9A × | Dash 10A ÷ | Dash 11A × | Dash 12A ÷ |
|---|---|---|---|---|---|---|---|
| a. 20 | a. 4 | a. 0 | a. 3 | a. 81 | a. 6 | a. 0 | a. 10 |
| b. 30 | b. 5 | b. 24 | b. 5 | b. 20 | b. 9 | b. 36 | b. 10 |
| c. 72 | c. 3 | c. 9 | c. 7 | c. 30 | c. 8 | c. 24 | c. 4 |
| d. 12 | d. 7 | d. 9 | d. 1 | d. 27 | d. 3 | d. 0 | d. 2 |
| e. 35 | e. 9 | e. 32 | e. 4 | e. 80 | e. 5 | e. 24 | e. 1 |
| f. 50 | f. 10 | f. 0 | f. 3 | f. 12 | f. 9 | f. 9 | f. 7 |
| g. 16 | g. 7 | g. 6 | g. 8 | g. 72 | g. 7 | g. 9 | g. 7 |
| h. 60 | h. 7 | h. 12 | h. 8 | h. 8 | h. 10 | h. 32 | h. 8 |
| i. 27 | i. 3 | i. 28 | i. 6 | i. 100 | i. 7 | i. 0 | i. 5 |
| j. 18 | j. 9 | j. 21 | j. 6 | j. 54 | j. 5 | j. 6 | j. 9 |
| k. 40 | k. 1 | k. 0 | k. 10 | k. 35 | k. 4 | k. 20 | k. 3 |
| l. 70 | l. 5 | l. 10 | l. 10 | l. 50 | l. 3 | l. 0 | l. 5 |
| m. 25 | m. 6 | m. 16 | m. 4 | m. 16 | m. 9 | m. 27 | m. 7 |
| n. 5 | n. 3 | n. 27 | n. 2 | n. 60 | n. 7 | n. 16 | n. 1 |
| o. 54 | o. 8 | o. 0 | o. 1 | o. 18 | o. 3 | o. 10 | o. 4 |
| p. 100 | p. 8 | p. 20 | p. 7 | p. 54 | p. 1 | p. 12 | p. 3 |
| q. 8 | q. 8 | q. 6 | q. 7 | q. 5 | q. 6 | q. 28 | q. 8 |
| r. 80 | r. 9 | r. 24 | r. 8 | r. 25 | r. 8 | r. 21 | r. 8 |
| s. 27 | s. 4 | s. 36 | s. 5 | s. 70 | s. 8 | s. 0 | s. 6 |
| t. 81 | t. 6 | t. 0 | t. 9 | t. 40 | t. 4 | t. 10 | t. 6 |

## ► Solve Word Problems with 2s, 3s, 4s, 5s, and 9s

**Write an equation and solve the problem.**          *Show your work.*

1. Toni counted 36 legs in the lion house at the zoo.
   How many lions were there?

   _____

2. One wall of an art gallery has a row of 5 paintings and a
   row of 9 paintings. How many paintings are on the wall?

   _____

3. Josh's muffin pan is an array with 4 rows and
   6 columns. How many muffins can Josh make in the pan?

   _____

4. To get ready for the school spelling bee, Tanya studied
   3 hours each night for an entire week. How many hours
   did she study?

   _____

5. The 14 trumpet players in the marching band lined up in
   2 equal rows. How many trumpet players were in each row?

   _____

6. The Sunnyside Riding Stable has 9 horses. The owners are
   going to buy new horseshoes for all the horses. How many
   horseshoes are needed?

   _____

## ► Make Sense of Problems

**Write an equation and solve the problem.**

*Show your work.*

7. Sadie plans to read 2 books every month for 6 months. How many books will she read during that time?

_____

8. A farmers' market sells pumpkins for $5 each. On Friday the market made $35 from the sale of pumpkins. How many pumpkins did the market sell on Friday?

_____

9. A keypad on Tim's phone has 21 buttons. There are 3 buttons in each row. How many rows of buttons are on the keypad?

_____

10. Paisley has a quilt that is made of different color squares. The quilt has 6 rows of 4 squares. How many squares are in the quilt?

_____

11. Each student collected 10 leaves for a group science project. If the group collected a total of 80 leaves, how many students are in the group?

_____

## ► Write a Word Problem

12. Write and solve a word problem that can be solved using the equation $4 \times 1 = n$.

_____

_____

_____

Building Fluency with 0s, 1s, 2s, 3s, 4s, 5s, 9s, and 10s

► PATH to FLUENCY **Math and Hobbies**

A hobby is something you do for fun. Owen's hobby is photography. He took pictures on a field trip and displayed them on a poster.

**Solve.**

1. How many photos did Owen display on the poster? Explain the different strategies you can use to find the answer. Write an equation for each.

_____

_____

_____

_____

2. What other ways could Owen have arranged the photos in an array on the poster?

_____

_____

► PATH to FLUENCY **What is Your Hobby?**

Carina asked some third graders, "What is your hobby?"
The answers are shown under the photos.

**Photography**
Eight more than dancing
said photography.

**Dancing**
Four third graders
said dancing.

**Reading**
Six less than photography said
reading.

**Games**
Eight third graders said
games.

**3.** **Use the information above to complete the chart below.**

What is Your Hobby?

| Hobby | Number of Students |
|---|---|
| Dancing | |
| Photography | |
| Games | |
| Reading | |

**4.** **Use the chart to complete the pictograph below.**

**Hobbies**

| | |
|---|---|
| Dancing | |
| Photography | |
| Games | |
| Reading | |

Each ☐ stands for 2 third graders.

**5.** How many third graders answered Carina's question?

_____

## ► Vocabulary

**Choose the best word from the box.**

1. Groups that have the same number of objects in each group are called _____. (Lesson 1-2)

2. When you multiply two numbers, the answer is the _____. (Lesson 1-1)

3. The 3 and 4 in $3 \times 4 = 12$ are called _____. (Lesson 1-1)

## ► Concepts and Skills

4. Explain three ways to find the area of the rectangle at the right. Use the ways to find the area. (Lesson 1-11)

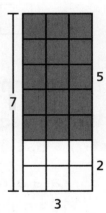

_____

_____

_____

_____

5. What pattern can you use to multiply a number and 9 if you know 10 times the number? Give an example. (Lesson 1-8)

_____

_____

**Write and solve a multiplication equation with an unknown to find the answer.** (Lessons 1-4, 1-5, 1-6, 1-7)

6. $18 \div \boxed{\phantom{0}} = 9$

7. $54 \div 9 = \boxed{\phantom{0}}$

## Multiply or divide.

(Lessons 1-1, 1-4, 1-5, 1-6, 1-7, 1-9, 1-10, 1-12, 1-14, 1-15, 1-18)

8. $8 \times 2 =$ ☐

9. $5 \cdot 7 =$ ☐

10. $10 \div 1 =$ ☐

11. $81 \div 9 =$ ☐

12. $4 \times 0 =$ ☐

13. $63/9 =$ ☐

14. $6 \cdot 4 =$ ☐

15. $45/5 =$ ☐

16. ☐ $3\overline{)24}$

17. ☐ $\times 3 = 27$

18. $28 \div$ ☐ $= 7$

19. $10 \cdot$ ☐ $= 80$

20. $6 \times$ ☐ $= 18$

21. $35/5 =$ ☐

22. ☐ $\times 6 = 30$

## ► Problem Solving

**Write an equation and solve the problem.** (Lessons 1-4, 1-5, 1-6, 1-7, 1-8, 1-9, 1-10, 1-12, 1-14, 1-15, 1-16, 1-18)

23. Zara arranged 80 stamps of her stamp collection in 10 equal rows. How many stamps were in each row?

_____

24. Olivia's CD rack has 4 shelves. It holds 8 CDs on a shelf. How many CDs will fit in the rack altogether?

_____

25. **Extended Response** Paco set up 7 tables to seat 28 children at his birthday party. The same number of children will sit at each table. How many children will sit at each table? Explain how you found your answer. Make a math drawing to help.

_____

_____

**Family Letter**

Dear Family,

In this unit, students learn multiplications and divisions for 6s, 7s, and 8s, while continuing to practice the rest of the basic multiplications and divisions covered in Unit 1.

Although students practice all the 6s, 7s, and 8s multiplications, they really have only six new multiplications to learn: 6 × 6, 6 × 7, 6 × 8, 7 × 7, 7 × 8, and 8 × 8. The lessons for these multiplications focus on strategies for finding the products using multiplications they know.

This unit also focuses on word problems. Students are presented with a variety of one-step and two-step word problems.

Here is an example of a two-step problem:

A roller coaster has 7 cars. Each car has 4 seats. If there were 3 empty seats, how many people were on the roller coaster?

Students use the language and context of each problem to determine which operation or operations—multiplication, division, addition, or subtraction—they must use to solve it. Students use a variety of methods to solve two-step word problems.

Please continue to help your child get faster on multiplications and divisions. Use all of the practice materials that your child has brought home. Your support is crucial to your child's learning.

Please call if you have any questions or comments.

Thank you.

Sincerely,
Your child's teacher

**COMMON CORE**

This unit includes the Common Core Standards for Mathematical Content for Operations and Algebraic Thinking, 3.OA.1, 3.OA.2, 3.OA.3, 3.OA.4, 3.OA.5, 3.OA.6, 3.OA.7, 3.OA.8, 3.OA.9; Number and Operations in Base Ten, 3.NBT.3; Measurement and Data, 3.MD.5a, 3.MD.5b, 3.MD.7a, 3.MD.7b and all Mathematical Practices

Estimada familia:

En esta unidad los estudiantes aprenden las multiplicaciones y divisiones con el 6, el 7 y el 8, mientras siguen practicando las demás multiplicaciones y divisiones que se presentaron en la Unidad 1.

Aunque los estudiantes practican todas las multiplicaciones con el 6, el 7 y el 8, en realidad sólo tienen que aprender seis multiplicaciones nuevas: $6 \times 6$, $6 \times 7$, $6 \times 8$, $7 \times 7$, $7 \times 8$ y $8 \times 8$. Las lecciones acerca de estas multiplicaciones se centran en estrategias para hallar los productos usando multiplicaciones que ya se conocen.

Esta unidad también se centra en problemas verbales. A los estudiantes se les presenta una variedad de problemas de uno y de dos pasos.

Este es un ejemplo de un problema de dos pasos:
Una montaña rusa tiene 7 carros. Cada carro tiene 7 asientos. Si hay 3 asientos vacíos. Cuántas personas había en la montaña rusa?

Los estudiantes aprovechan el lenguaje y el contexto de cada problema para determinar qué operación u operaciones deben usar para resolverlo: multiplicación, división, suma o resta. Los estudiantes usan una variedad de métodos para resolver problemas de dos pasos.

Por favor continúe ayudando a su niño a practicar las multiplicaciones y las divisiones. Use todos los materiales de práctica que su niño ha llevado a casa. Su apoyo es importante para el aprendizaje de su niño.

Si tiene alguna duda o pregunta, por favor comuníquese conmigo.

Atentamente,
El maestro de su niño

COMMON CORE

Esta unidad incluye los Common Core Standards for Mathematical Content for Operations and Algebraic Thinking, 3.OA.1, 3.OA.2, 3.OA.3, 3.OA.4, 3.OA.5, 3.OA.6, 3.OA.7, 3.OA.8, 3.OA.9; Number and Operations in Base Ten, 3.NBT.3; Measurement and Data, 3.MD.5a, 3.MD.5b, 3.MD.7a, 3.MD.7b and all Mathematical Practices

Multiply and Divide with 6

► PATH to FLUENCY **Explore Patterns with 6s**

## What patterns do you see below?

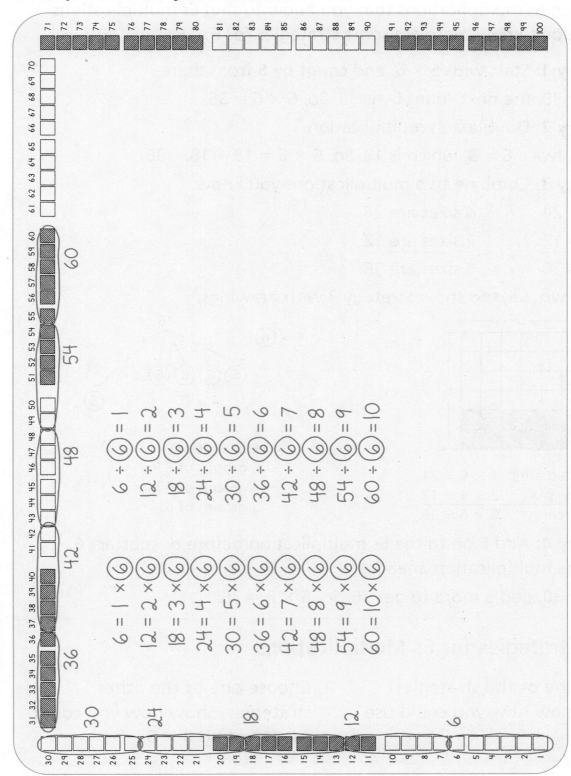

PATH to
FLUENCY

► **Strategies for Multiplying with 6**

You can use 6s multiplications that you know to find 6s multiplications that you don't know. Here are some strategies for $6 \times 6$.

- **Strategy 1:** Start with $5 \times 6$, and count by 6 from there.

  $5 \times 6 = 30$, the next count by is 36. So, $6 \times 6 = 36$.

- **Strategy 2:** Double a 3s multiplication.

  $6 \times 6$ is twice $6 \times 3$, which is 18. So, $6 \times 6 = 18 + 18 = 36$.

- **Strategy 3:** Combine two multiplications you know.

  | | |
  |---|---|
  | $4 \times 6 = 24$ | 4 sixes are 24. |
  | $2 \times 6 = 12$ | 2 sixes are 12. |
  | $6 \times 6 = 36$ | 6 sixes are 36. |

Here are two ways to show Strategy 3 with drawings.

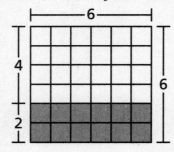

unshaded area: $4 \times 6 = 24$
shaded area: $\quad 2 \times 6 = 12$
total area: $\quad\quad 6 \times 6 = 36$

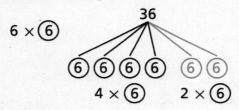

**Explanation:**
6 groups of 6 is
4 groups of 6 plus
2 groups of 6.

- **Strategy 4:** Add 6 on to the 6s multiplication before or subtract 6 from the multiplication ahead.

  $5 \times 6 = 30$, add 6 more to get 36. So, $6 \times 6 = 36$.

► **Apply Strategies for 6s Multiplications**

1. Choose one of the strategies above. Show how you could use it to find $7 \times 6$.

2. Choose one of the other strategies. Show how you could use it to find $8 \times 6$.

**Name** _____  **Date** _____

## Study Sheet C

### 7s

| Count-bys | Mixed Up × | Mixed Up ÷ |
|---|---|---|
| 1 × 7 = 7 | 6 × 7 = 42 | 70 ÷ 7 = 10 |
| 2 × 7 = 14 | 8 × 7 = 56 | 14 ÷ 7 = 2 |
| 3 × 7 = 21 | 5 × 7 = 35 | 28 ÷ 7 = 4 |
| 4 × 7 = 28 | 9 × 7 = 63 | 56 ÷ 7 = 8 |
| 5 × 7 = 35 | 4 × 7 = 28 | 42 ÷ 7 = 6 |
| 6 × 7 = 42 | 10 × 7 = 70 | 63 ÷ 7 = 9 |
| 7 × 7 = 49 | 3 × 7 = 21 | 21 ÷ 7 = 3 |
| 8 × 7 = 56 | 1 × 7 = 7 | 49 ÷ 7 = 7 |
| 9 × 7 = 63 | 7 × 7 = 49 | 7 ÷ 7 = 1 |
| 10 × 7 = 70 | 2 × 7 = 14 | 35 ÷ 7 = 5 |

### Squares

| Count-bys | Mixed Up × | Mixed Up ÷ |
|---|---|---|
| 1 × 1 = 1 | 3 × 3 = 9 | 25 ÷ 5 = 5 |
| 2 × 2 = 4 | 9 × 9 = 81 | 4 ÷ 2 = 2 |
| 3 × 3 = 9 | 4 × 4 = 16 | 81 ÷ 9 = 9 |
| 4 × 4 = 16 | 6 × 6 = 36 | 9 ÷ 3 = 3 |
| 5 × 5 = 25 | 2 × 2 = 4 | 36 ÷ 6 = 6 |
| 6 × 6 = 36 | 7 × 7 = 49 | 100 ÷ 10 = 10 |
| 7 × 7 = 49 | 10 × 10 = 100 | 16 ÷ 4 = 4 |
| 8 × 8 = 64 | 1 × 1 = 1 | 49 ÷ 7 = 7 |
| 9 × 9 = 81 | 5 × 5 = 25 | 1 ÷ 1 = 1 |
| 10 × 10 = 100 | 8 × 8 = 64 | 64 ÷ 8 = 8 |

### 6s

| Count-bys | Mixed Up × | Mixed Up ÷ |
|---|---|---|
| 1 × 6 = 6 | 10 × 6 = 60 | 54 ÷ 6 = 9 |
| 2 × 6 = 12 | 8 × 6 = 48 | 30 ÷ 6 = 5 |
| 3 × 6 = 18 | 2 × 6 = 12 | 12 ÷ 6 = 2 |
| 4 × 6 = 24 | 6 × 6 = 36 | 60 ÷ 6 = 10 |
| 5 × 6 = 30 | 4 × 6 = 24 | 48 ÷ 6 = 8 |
| 6 × 6 = 36 | 1 × 6 = 6 | 36 ÷ 6 = 6 |
| 7 × 6 = 42 | 9 × 6 = 54 | 6 ÷ 6 = 1 |
| 8 × 6 = 48 | 3 × 6 = 18 | 42 ÷ 6 = 7 |
| 9 × 6 = 54 | 7 × 6 = 42 | 18 ÷ 6 = 3 |
| 10 × 6 = 60 | 5 × 6 = 30 | 24 ÷ 6 = 4 |

### 8s

| Count-bys | Mixed Up × | Mixed Up ÷ |
|---|---|---|
| 1 × 8 = 8 | 6 × 8 = 48 | 16 ÷ 8 = 2 |
| 2 × 8 = 16 | 10 × 8 = 80 | 40 ÷ 8 = 5 |
| 3 × 8 = 24 | 7 × 8 = 56 | 72 ÷ 8 = 9 |
| 4 × 8 = 32 | 2 × 8 = 16 | 32 ÷ 8 = 4 |
| 5 × 8 = 40 | 4 × 8 = 32 | 8 ÷ 8 = 1 |
| 6 × 8 = 48 | 8 × 8 = 64 | 80 ÷ 8 = 10 |
| 7 × 8 = 56 | 5 × 8 = 40 | 64 ÷ 8 = 8 |
| 8 × 8 = 64 | 9 × 8 = 72 | 24 ÷ 8 = 3 |
| 9 × 8 = 72 | 3 × 8 = 24 | 56 ÷ 8 = 7 |
| 10 × 8 = 80 | 1 × 8 = 8 | 48 ÷ 8 = 6 |

► **PATH to FLUENCY** **Unknown Number Puzzles**

## Complete each Unknown Number puzzle.

**1.**

| × | 5 | 2 | |
|---|---|---|---|
| | 30 | | 48 |
| 4 | | 8 | 32 |
| | 45 | | 72 |

**2.**

| × | | 3 | |
|---|---|---|---|
| 6 | 30 | | 42 |
| 4 | | | 28 |
| | 40 | 24 | 56 |

**3.**

| × | 4 | | 8 |
|---|---|---|---|
| 9 | | 81 | |
| | 12 | | 24 |
| | 20 | 45 | 40 |

**4.**

| × | | 3 | |
|---|---|---|---|
| | 60 | | 20 |
| 6 | 36 | | |
| | 18 | 9 | 6 |

**5.**

| × | 8 | | 2 |
|---|---|---|---|
| 7 | | 28 | |
| | | 16 | 8 |
| | 32 | 16 | 8 |

**6.**

| × | 9 | | |
|---|---|---|---|
| 8 | | 56 | 24 |
| | 54 | 42 | 18 |
| 5 | | | 15 |

**7.**

| × | 8 | | 7 |
|---|---|---|---|
| 8 | | 40 | |
| | 32 | 20 | 28 |
| | 24 | 15 | |

**8.**

| × | 3 | 4 | |
|---|---|---|---|
| | 27 | 36 | 81 |
| 7 | | | 63 |
| | | | 18 |

**9.**

| × | | | 10 |
|---|---|---|---|
| 8 | 48 | 16 | |
| 7 | 42 | 14 | |
| | 36 | | 60 |

# ► Tiling and Multiplying to Find Area

**Use inch tiles to find the area. Then label the side lengths and find the area using multiplication.**

10.

Area: _____ _____

11.

Area: _____ _____

12.

Area: _____ _____

13.

Area: _____ _____

*Show your work.*

# ▶ Draw Rectangles to Solve Area Word Problems

**Draw a rectangle to help solve each problem.**
**Label your answers with the correct units.**

**14.** The mattress has a length of 7 feet and a width of 6 feet. What is the area of the mattress?

_____

**15.** The wading pool at Evans Park is shaped like a square with sides 8 feet long. What is the area of the wading pool?

_____

**16.** Milo's rug has a length of 5 feet and an area of 40 square feet. What is the width of his rug?

_____

**17.** Lana wants to enclose a garden plot. Each side of the garden will be 9 feet. What is the area of the garden?

_____

**18.** A picture has a length of 6 inches and a width of 8 inches. What is the area of the picture?

_____

**19.** A quilt square has sides that are 7 inches long. What is the area of the quilt square?

_____

# ▶ Draw a Picture to Solve a Problem

**Draw a picture to help solve each problem.**

20. Ana has a ribbon that is 18 inches long.
She cut the ribbon into 3 equal pieces.
Then she cut each of those pieces in half.
How many small pieces of ribbon are there?
How long is each piece?

    _____

21. A sign is shaped like a square. Eva draws lines
on the sign to make 3 equal rectangles. Each
rectangle is 3 inches wide and 9 inches long.
What is the area of the square?

    _____

22. Ty uses 20 feet of fencing to make a rectangular
garden. He divides the rectangle into 4 equal
squares all in one row. The side of each square
is 2 feet long. What is the area of the garden?

    _____

23. Aaron is stacking cans in a grocery store. The
bottom row has 7 cans. Each row above has 1
fewer can. How many cans will be stacked in all?

    _____

24. There are 4 cars in a row. Each car is 13 feet
long. There are 6 feet between each car. What
is the length from the front of the first car to
the back of the last car in the row?

    _____

► **PATH to FLUENCY** **Check Sheet 7: 6s and 8s**

| 6s Multiplications | 6s Divisions | 8s Multiplications | 8s Divisions |
|---|---|---|---|
| $10 \times 6 = 60$ | $24 / 6 = 4$ | $2 \times 8 = 16$ | $72 / 8 = 9$ |
| $6 \cdot 4 = 24$ | $48 \div 6 = 8$ | $8 \cdot 10 = 80$ | $16 \div 8 = 2$ |
| $6 * 7 = 42$ | $60 / 6 = 10$ | $3 * 8 = 24$ | $40 / 8 = 5$ |
| $2 \times 6 = 12$ | $12 \div 6 = 2$ | $9 \times 8 = 72$ | $8 \div 8 = 1$ |
| $6 \cdot 5 = 30$ | $42 / 6 = 7$ | $8 \cdot 4 = 32$ | $80 / 8 = 10$ |
| $6 * 8 = 48$ | $30 \div 6 = 5$ | $8 * 7 = 56$ | $48 \div 8 = 6$ |
| $9 \times 6 = 54$ | $6 / 6 = 1$ | $5 \times 8 = 40$ | $56 / 8 = 7$ |
| $6 \cdot 1 = 6$ | $18 \div 6 = 3$ | $8 \cdot 6 = 48$ | $24 \div 8 = 3$ |
| $6 * 6 = 36$ | $54 / 6 = 9$ | $1 * 8 = 8$ | $64 / 8 = 8$ |
| $6 \times 3 = 18$ | $36 / 6 = 6$ | $8 \times 8 = 64$ | $32 / 8 = 4$ |
| $6 \cdot 6 = 36$ | $48 \div 6 = 8$ | $4 \cdot 8 = 32$ | $80 \div 8 = 10$ |
| $5 * 6 = 30$ | $12 / 6 = 2$ | $6 * 8 = 48$ | $56 / 8 = 7$ |
| $6 \times 2 = 12$ | $24 \div 6 = 4$ | $8 \times 3 = 24$ | $8 \div 8 = 1$ |
| $4 \cdot 6 = 24$ | $60 / 6 = 10$ | $7 \cdot 8 = 56$ | $24 / 8 = 3$ |
| $6 * 9 = 54$ | $6 \div 6 = 1$ | $8 * 2 = 16$ | $64 \div 8 = 8$ |
| $8 \times 6 = 48$ | $42 / 6 = 7$ | $8 \times 9 = 72$ | $16 / 8 = 2$ |
| $7 \cdot 6 = 42$ | $18 \div 6 = 3$ | $8 \cdot 1 = 8$ | $72 \div 8 = 9$ |
| $6 * 10 = 60$ | $36 \div 6 = 6$ | $8 * 8 = 64$ | $32 \div 8 = 4$ |
| $1 \times 6 = 6$ | $30 / 6 = 5$ | $10 \times 8 = 80$ | $40 / 8 = 5$ |
| $4 \cdot 6 = 24$ | $54 \div 6 = 9$ | $5 \cdot 8 = 40$ | $48 \div 8 = 6$ |

► PATH to FLUENCY **Explore Patterns with 8s**

## What patterns do you see below?

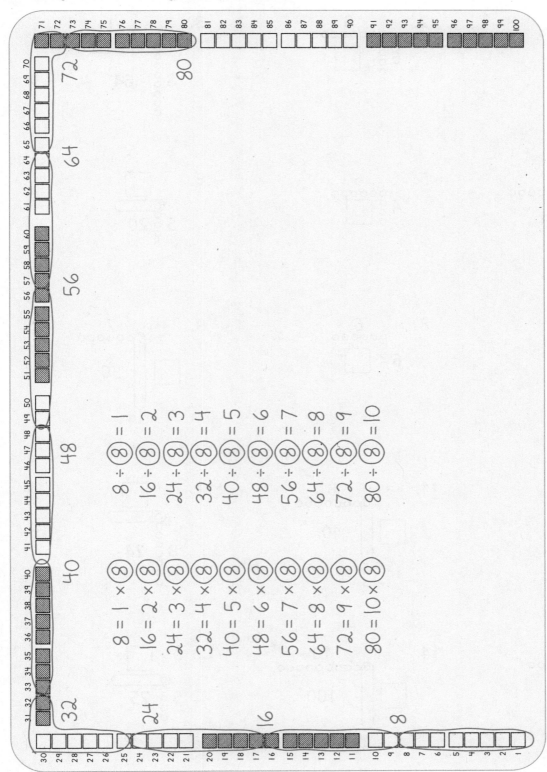

► **PATH to FLUENCY** **Fast-Array Drawings**

## Find the unknown number for each Fast-Array drawing.

1.   6
□ 42

2.   8
6 □

3.   □
8  64

4.   9
□ 63

5.   6
4 □

6.   □
5  20

7.   □
9  45

8.   6
6 □

9.   7
□  56

10.  7
7 □

11.  8
□  40

12.  □
8  24

13.  9
8 □

14.  10
□  100

15.  □
5  25

Multiply and Divide with 8

## ► Identify the Type and Choose the Operation

**Solve. Then circle what type it is and what operation you use.**

1. Students in Mr. Till's class hung their paintings on the wall. They made 6 rows, with 5 paintings in each row. How many paintings did the students hang?

   _____

   **Circle one:**    array        equal groups          area
   **Circle one:**    multiplication     division

2. Write your own problem that is the same type as problem 1. _____

   _____

   _____

3. There are 8 goldfish in each tank at the pet store. If there are 56 goldfish in all, how many tanks are there?

   _____

   **Circle one:**    array        equal groups          area
   **Circle one:**    multiplication        division

4. Write your own problem that is the same type as problem 3. _____

   _____

   _____

5. Pierre built a rectangular pen for his rabbits. The pen is 4 feet wide and 6 feet long. What is the area of the pen? _____

   **Circle one:**    array        equal groups          area
   **Circle one:**    multiplication        division

Name _____    Date _____

## ► Identify the Type and Choose the Operation (continued)

6. Write your own problem that is the same type as problem 5. _____

_____

_____

_____

7. Paulo arranged 72 baseball cards in 9 rows and a certain number of columns. Into how many columns did he arrange the cards? _____

   **Circle one:**  array        equal groups           area
   **Circle one:**  multiplication    division

8. Write your own problem that is the same type as Problem 7. _____

_____

_____

_____

9. The store sells bottles of juice in six-packs. Mr. Lee bought 9 six-packs for a picnic. How many bottles did he buy? _____

   **Circle one:**  array        equal groups           area
   **Circle one:**  multiplication    division

10. Write your own problem that is the same type as Problem 9. _____

_____

_____

_____

11. **Math Journal** Write an area multiplication problem. Draw a Fast Array to solve it.

## ▶ What's the Error?

Dear Math Students,

Today my teacher asked me to find the answer to 8 x 6. Here is what I wrote:

8 x 6 = 14

Is my answer correct? If not, please correct my work and tell me what I did wrong.

Your friend,
Puzzled Penguin

**12.** Write an answer to the Puzzled Penguin.

_____

_____

## ▶ Write and Solve Equations

**Write an equation and solve the problem.**

**13.** A large box of crayons holds 60 crayons. There are 10 crayons in each row. How many rows are there?

_____

**14.** A poster covers 12 square feet. The poster is 4 feet long. How wide is the poster?

_____

**15.** There are 7 groups of students with an equal number of students in each group working on a social studies project. There are 28 students working on the project. How many students are there in each group?

_____

**16.** Amanda has 15 bracelets. She gave a number of bracelets to friends. She has 10 bracelets left. How many bracelets did she give to friends?

_____

# ► Write and Solve Equations (continued)

**Write an equation and solve the problem.**

17. John has 24 baseball cards. He divided them equally among 6 friends. How many cards did each friend get?

_____

18. A third grade class of 24 students has 14 girls in it. How many boys are in the class?

_____

19. There are 16 pencils left in a container. Eight students will divide the pencils equally. How many pencils will each student get?

_____

20. Marc bought 18 golf balls. The golf balls were packaged in boxes of 6. How many boxes of golf balls did Marc buy?

_____

21. Lara keeps her DVDs in a case that has 10 sleeves. Each sleeve can hold 6 DVDs. How many DVDs can the case hold?

_____

22. Write a problem that can be solved using the equation $54 \div 6 = n$, where $n$ is the number in each group. Then solve the problem.

_____

_____

Write Word Problems and Equations

► PATH to FLUENCY **Explore Patterns with 7s**

## What patterns do you see below?

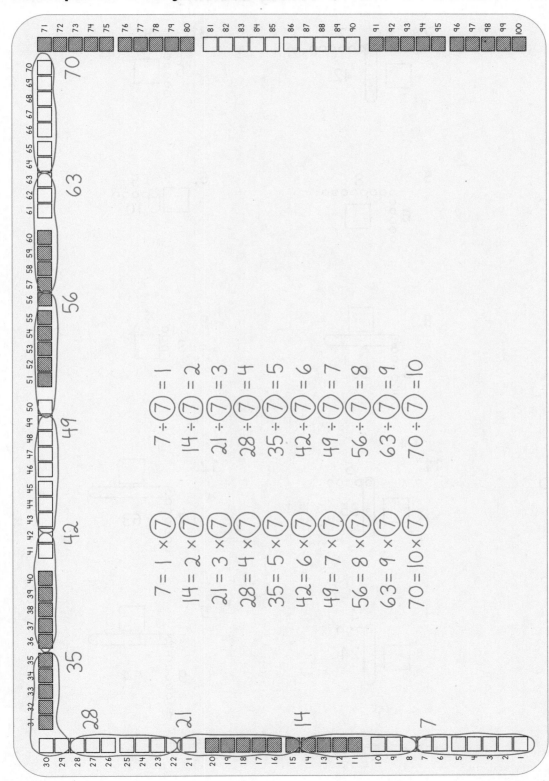

$7 \div 7 = 1$
$14 \div 7 = 2$
$21 \div 7 = 3$
$28 \div 7 = 4$
$35 \div 7 = 5$
$42 \div 7 = 6$
$49 \div 7 = 7$
$56 \div 7 = 8$
$63 \div 7 = 9$
$70 \div 7 = 10$

$7 = 1 \times 7$
$14 = 2 \times 7$
$21 = 3 \times 7$
$28 = 4 \times 7$
$35 = 5 \times 7$
$42 = 6 \times 7$
$49 = 7 \times 7$
$56 = 8 \times 7$
$63 = 9 \times 7$
$70 = 10 \times 7$

Name _____     Date _____

► PATH to FLUENCY **More Fast-Array Drawings**

## Find the unknown number for each Fast-Array Drawing.

1.   7
4 □

2.   7
□ 42

3.   5
6 □

4.   □
3 24

5.   8
6 □

6.   5
□ 10

7.   6
□ 36

8.   □
8 56

9.   4
3 □

10.   7
7 □

11.   5
□ 35

12.   □
7 63

13.   6
8 □

14.   4
□ 24

15.   □
9 54

Multiply and Divide with 7

▶ **PATH to FLUENCY** **Check Sheet 8: 7s and Squares**

| 7s Multiplications | 7s Divisions | Squares Multiplications | Squares Divisions |
|---|---|---|---|
| 4 × 7 = 28 | 14 / 7 = 2 | 8 × 8 = 64 | 81 / 9 = 9 |
| 7 • 2 = 14 | 28 ÷ 7 = 4 | 10 • 10 = 100 | 4 ÷ 2 = 2 |
| 7 * 8 = 56 | 70 / 7 = 10 | 3 * 3 = 9 | 25 / 5 = 5 |
| 7 × 7 = 49 | 56 ÷ 7 = 8 | 9 × 9 = 81 | 1 ÷ 1 = 1 |
| 7 • 1 = 7 | 42 / 7 = 6 | 4 • 4 = 16 | 100 / 10 = 10 |
| 7 * 10 = 70 | 63 ÷ 7 = 9 | 7 * 7 = 49 | 36 ÷ 6 = 6 |
| 3 × 7 = 21 | 7 / 7 = 1 | 5 × 5 = 25 | 49 / 7 = 7 |
| 7 • 6 = 42 | 49 ÷ 7 = 7 | 6 • 6 = 36 | 9 ÷ 3 = 3 |
| 5 * 7 = 35 | 21 / 7 = 3 | 1 * 1 = 1 | 64 / 8 = 8 |
| 7 × 9 = 63 | 35 / 7 = 5 | 5 * 5 = 25 | 16 / 4 = 4 |
| 7 • 4 = 28 | 7 ÷ 7 = 1 | 1 • 1 = 1 | 100 ÷ 10 = 10 |
| 9 * 7 = 63 | 63 / 7 = 9 | 3 • 3 = 9 | 49 / 7 = 7 |
| 2 × 7 = 14 | 14 ÷ 7 = 2 | 10 × 10 = 100 | 1 ÷ 1 = 1 |
| 7 • 5 = 35 | 70 / 7 = 10 | 4 × 4 = 16 | 9 / 3 = 3 |
| 8 * 7 = 56 | 21 ÷ 7 = 3 | 9 * 9 = 81 | 64 ÷ 8 = 8 |
| 7 × 3 = 21 | 49 / 7 = 7 | 2 × 2 = 4 | 4 / 2 = 2 |
| 6 • 7 = 42 | 28 ÷ 7 = 4 | 6 * 6 = 36 | 81 ÷ 9 = 9 |
| 10 * 7 = 70 | 56 ÷ 7 = 8 | 7 × 7 = 49 | 16 ÷ 4 = 4 |
| 1 × 7 = 7 | 35 / 7 = 5 | 5 • 5 = 25 | 25 / 5 = 5 |
| 7 • 7 = 49 | 42 ÷ 7 = 6 | 8 • 8 = 64 | 36 ÷ 6 = 6 |

Check Sheet 8: 7s and Squares

► PATH to FLUENCY **Explore Square Numbers**

## Write an equation to show the area of each large square.

**1.** $1 \times 1 = 1$     **2.** _____     **3.** _____     **4.** _____

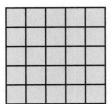 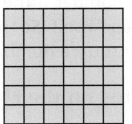

**5.** _____     **6.** _____

 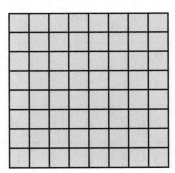

**7.** _____     **8.** _____

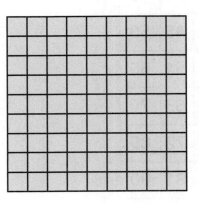 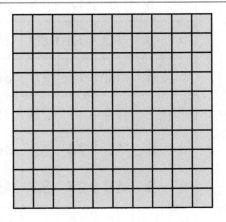

**9.** _____     **10.** _____

VOCABULARY
square numbers

## ▶ Look for Patterns

**11.** List the products in Exercises 1–10 in order.
Discuss the patterns you see with your class.

_____

The numbers you listed in Exercise 11 are called
**square numbers** because they are the areas of
squares with whole-number lengths of sides.
A square number is the product of a whole
number and itself. So, if $n$ is a whole number,
$n \times n$ is a square number.

## ▶ Patterns on the Multiplication Table

**12.** In the table below, circle the products that are
square numbers. Discuss the patterns you see
with your class.

| X | 1 | 2 | 3 | 4 | 5 | 6 | 7 | 8 | 9 | 10 |
|----|----|----|----|----|----|----|----|----|----|----|
| 1 | 1 | 2 | 3 | 4 | 5 | 6 | 7 | 8 | 9 | 10 |
| 2 | 2 | 4 | 6 | 8 | 10 | 12 | 14 | 16 | 18 | 20 |
| 3 | 3 | 6 | 9 | 12 | 15 | 18 | 21 | 24 | 27 | 30 |
| 4 | 4 | 8 | 12 | 16 | 20 | 24 | 28 | 32 | 36 | 40 |
| 5 | 5 | 10 | 15 | 20 | 25 | 30 | 35 | 40 | 45 | 50 |
| 6 | 6 | 12 | 18 | 24 | 30 | 36 | 42 | 48 | 54 | 60 |
| 7 | 7 | 14 | 21 | 28 | 35 | 42 | 49 | 56 | 63 | 70 |
| 8 | 8 | 16 | 24 | 32 | 40 | 48 | 56 | 64 | 72 | 80 |
| 9 | 9 | 18 | 27 | 36 | 45 | 54 | 63 | 72 | 81 | 90 |
| 10 | 10 | 20 | 30 | 40 | 50 | 60 | 70 | 80 | 90 | 100 |

**Name** _____ **Date** _____

► PATH to FLUENCY **Check Sheet 9: 6s, 7s, and 8s**

| 6s, 7s, and 8s Multiplications | 6s, 7s, and 8s Multiplications | 6s, 7s, and 8s Divisions | 6s, 7s, and 8s Divisions |
|---|---|---|---|
| $1 \times 6 = 6$ | $0 \times 8 = 0$ | $24 / 6 = 4$ | $54 / 6 = 9$ |
| $6 \cdot 7 = 42$ | $6 \cdot 2 = 12$ | $21 \div 7 = 3$ | $24 \div 8 = 3$ |
| $3 * 8 = 24$ | $4 * 7 = 28$ | $16 / 8 = 2$ | $14 / 7 = 2$ |
| $6 \times 2 = 12$ | $8 \times 3 = 24$ | $24 \div 8 = 3$ | $32 \div 8 = 4$ |
| $7 \cdot 5 = 35$ | $5 \cdot 6 = 30$ | $14 / 7 = 2$ | $18 / 6 = 3$ |
| $8 * 4 = 32$ | $7 * 2 = 14$ | $30 \div 6 = 5$ | $56 \div 7 = 8$ |
| $6 \times 6 = 36$ | $3 \times 8 = 24$ | $35 / 7 = 5$ | $40 / 8 = 5$ |
| $8 \cdot 7 = 56$ | $6 \cdot 4 = 24$ | $24 \div 8 = 3$ | $35 \div 7 = 5$ |
| $9 * 8 = 72$ | $0 * 7 = 0$ | $18 / 6 = 3$ | $12 / 6 = 2$ |
| $6 \times 10 = 60$ | $8 \times 1 = 8$ | $12 / 6 = 2$ | $21 / 7 = 3$ |
| $7 \cdot 1 = 7$ | $8 \cdot 6 = 48$ | $42 \div 7 = 6$ | $16 \div 8 = 2$ |
| $8 * 3 = 24$ | $7 * 9 = 63$ | $56 / 8 = 7$ | $42 / 6 = 7$ |
| $5 \times 6 = 30$ | $10 \times 8 = 80$ | $49 \div 7 = 7$ | $80 \div 8 = 10$ |
| $4 \cdot 7 = 28$ | $6 \cdot 10 = 60$ | $16 / 8 = 2$ | $36 / 6 = 6$ |
| $2 * 8 = 16$ | $3 * 7 = 21$ | $60 \div 6 = 10$ | $7 \div 7 = 1$ |
| $7 \times 7 = 49$ | $8 \times 4 = 32$ | $54 / 6 = 9$ | $64 / 8 = 8$ |
| $7 \cdot 6 = 42$ | $6 \cdot 5 = 30$ | $8 \div 8 = 1$ | $24 \div 6 = 4$ |
| $8 * 8 = 64$ | $7 * 4 = 28$ | $28 \div 7 = 4$ | $21 \div 7 = 3$ |
| $9 \times 6 = 54$ | $8 \times 8 = 64$ | $72 / 8 = 9$ | $49 / 7 = 7$ |
| $10 \cdot 7 = 70$ | $6 \cdot 9 = 54$ | $56 \div 7 = 8$ | $24 \div 8 = 3$ |

**Name** _____  **Date** _____

► PATH to FLUENCY **Check Sheet 10: 0s–10s**

| 0s–10s Multiplications | 0s–10s Multiplications | 0s–10s Divisions | 0s–10s Divisions |
|---|---|---|---|
| $9 \times 0 = 0$ | $9 \times 4 = 36$ | $9 / 1 = 9$ | $90 / 10 = 9$ |
| $1 \cdot 1 = 1$ | $5 \cdot 9 = 45$ | $12 \div 3 = 4$ | $64 \div 8 = 8$ |
| $2 * 3 = 6$ | $6 * 10 = 60$ | $14 / 2 = 7$ | $15 / 5 = 3$ |
| $1 \times 3 = 3$ | $7 \times 3 = 21$ | $20 \div 4 = 5$ | $12 \div 6 = 2$ |
| $5 \cdot 4 = 20$ | $5 \cdot 3 = 15$ | $10 / 5 = 2$ | $14 / 7 = 2$ |
| $7 * 5 = 35$ | $4 * 1 = 4$ | $48 \div 8 = 6$ | $45 \div 9 = 5$ |
| $6 \times 9 = 54$ | $7 \times 5 = 35$ | $35 / 7 = 5$ | $8 / 1 = 8$ |
| $4 \cdot 7 = 28$ | $6 \cdot 3 = 18$ | $60 \div 6 = 10$ | $30 \div 3 = 10$ |
| $1 * 8 = 8$ | $8 * 7 = 56$ | $81 / 9 = 9$ | $16 / 4 = 4$ |
| $9 \times 8 = 72$ | $5 \times 8 = 40$ | $20 / 10 = 2$ | $8 / 2 = 4$ |
| $2 \cdot 10 = 20$ | $9 \cdot 9 = 81$ | $16 \div 2 = 8$ | $80 \div 10 = 8$ |
| $0 * 7 = 0$ | $9 * 10 = 90$ | $30 / 5 = 6$ | $36 / 4 = 9$ |
| $4 \times 1 = 4$ | $0 \times 0 = 0$ | $49 \div 7 = 7$ | $25 \div 5 = 5$ |
| $2 \cdot 4 = 8$ | $1 \cdot 0 = 0$ | $60 / 6 = 10$ | $42 / 7 = 6$ |
| $10 * 3 = 30$ | $1 * 6 = 6$ | $30 \div 3 = 10$ | $36 \div 6 = 6$ |
| $8 \times 4 = 32$ | $7 \times 2 = 14$ | $8 / 1 = 8$ | $90 / 9 = 10$ |
| $5 \cdot 8 = 40$ | $6 \cdot 3 = 18$ | $16 \div 4 = 4$ | $24 \div 8 = 3$ |
| $4 * 6 = 24$ | $4 * 5 = 20$ | $16 \div 8 = 2$ | $6 \div 2 = 3$ |
| $7 \times 6 = 42$ | $6 \times 6 = 36$ | $40 / 10 = 4$ | $9 / 3 = 3$ |
| $1 \cdot 8 = 8$ | $10 \cdot 7 = 70$ | $36 \div 9 = 4$ | $1 \div 1 = 1$ |

Check Sheet 10: 0s–10s

► **PATH to FLUENCY** **Play Quotient Match and Division Blockout**

**Read the rules for playing a game.**
**Then play the game with your partner.**

---

*Rules for Quotient Match*

Number of players: 2 or 3

What each player will need: Division Strategy Cards for 6s, 7s, and 8s

1. Shuffle the cards. Put the division cards, without answers side up, on the table in 6 rows of 4.

2. Players take turns. On each turn, a player chooses three cards that he or she thinks have the same quotient and turns them over.

3. If all three cards do have the same quotient the player takes them. If the cards do not have the same quotient, the player turns them back over so the without answers side is up.

4. Play continues until no cards remain.

*Rules for Division Blockout*

Number of players: 3

What each player will need: Blockout Game Board (TRB M70), Division Strategy Cards for 6s, 7s, and 8s

1. Players do not write anything on the game board. The first row is for 6s, the second row for 7s, and the third row for 8s, as indicated in the gray column on the left.

2. Each player shuffles his or her Division Strategy Cards for 6s, 7s, 8s, making sure the division sides without answers are up.

3. Repeat Steps 2, 3, and 4 above. This time players will place the Strategy Cards in the appropriate row to indicate whether the unknown factor is 6, 7, or 8.

---

► (PATH to FLUENCY) **Play Multiplication Blockout**

**Read the rules for playing *Multiplication Blockout*. Then play the game with your partner.**

---

**Rules for *Multiplication Block Out***

Number of players: 3

What each player will need: *Blockout* Game Board (TRB M70), Multiplication Strategy Cards for 6s, 7s, and 8s

1. Players choose any 5 factors from 2–9 and write them in any order in the gray spaces at the top of the game board. The players then write the products in the large white spaces. The result will be a scrambled multiplication table.

2. Once the table is complete, players cut off the gray row and gray column that show the factors so that only the products are showing. This will be the game board.

3. Each player shuffles his or her Multiplication Strategy Cards for 6s, 7s, and 8s, making sure the multiplication sides without answers are facing up.

4. One player says, "Go!" and everyone quickly places their Strategy Cards on the game board spaces showing the corresponding products. When a player's game board is completely filled, he or she shouts, "Blockout!"

5. Everyone stops and checks the player's work. If all the cards are placed correctly, that player is the winner. If the player has made a mistake, he or she sits out and waits for the next player to shout, "Blockout!"

---

PATH to
FLUENCY

## ▶ Solve Word Problems with 6s, 7s, 8s

**Write an equation and solve the problem.**

1. Terri counted 32 legs in the lion house at the zoo. How many lions were there?

   _____

2. Kyle saw 9 ladybugs while he was camping. Each one had 6 legs. How many legs did the 9 ladybugs have in all?

   _____

3. Adam walks 3 miles a day. How many miles does he walk in a week?

   _____

4. Nancy's dog Rover eats 6 cups of food a day. In 8 days, how many cups of food does Rover eat?

   _____

5. The school library has 72 books on the topic of weather. If 8 students shared the books equally, how many books would each student receive?

   _____

6. The 42 trumpet players in the marching band lined up in 6 equal rows. How many trumpet players were in each row?

   _____

## ▶ Solve Word Problems with 6s, 7s, and 8s (continued)

**Write an equation and solve the problem.**

7. Susan is having a party. She has 18 cups. She puts them in 6 equal stacks. How many cups are in each stack?

   _____

8. Regina made an array with 7 rows of 9 blocks. How many blocks are in the array?

   _____

9. Mr. Rodriguez plans to invite 40 students to a picnic. The invitations come in packs of 8. How many packs of invitations does Mr. Rodriguez need to buy?

   _____

10. A classroom has 7 rows of 4 desks. How many desks are there in the classroom?

    _____

11. Write a word problem for $48 \div 6$ where 6 is the size of the group.

    _____

    _____

12. Write a word problem for $7 \times 9$ where 9 is the number of items in the collection.

    _____

    _____

► PATH to FLUENCY **Complete a Multiplication Table**

1. Look at the factors to complete the Multiplication Table.
   Leave blanks for the products you do not know.

| ✕ | 1 | 2 | 3 | 4 | 5 | 6 | 7 | 8 | 9 | 10 |
|---|---|---|---|---|---|---|---|---|---|----|
| 1 | | | | | | | | | | |
| 2 | | | | | | | | | | |
| 3 | | | | | | | | | | |
| 4 | | | | | | | | | | |
| 5 | | | | | | | | | | |
| 6 | | | | | | | | | | |
| 7 | | | | | | | | | | |
| 8 | | | | | | | | | | |
| 9 | | | | | | | | | | |
| 10 | | | | | | | | | | |

2. Write the multiplications you need to practice.

_____

_____

_____

_____

_____

_____

**Name** _____  **Date** _____

► PATH to FLUENCY **Scrambled Multiplication Tables**

The factors are at the side and top of each table.
The products are in the white boxes.

**Complete each table.**

**A**

| × | | | | | | | | | | |
|---|---|---|---|---|---|---|---|---|---|---|
| | 6 | 30 | 54 | 60 | 42 | 24 | 18 | 12 | 48 | 36 |
| | 2 | 10 | 18 | 20 | 14 | 8 | 6 | 4 | 16 | 12 |
| | 10 | 50 | 90 | 100 | 70 | 40 | 30 | 20 | 80 | 60 |
| | 8 | 40 | 72 | 80 | 56 | 32 | 24 | 16 | 64 | 48 |
| | 5 | 25 | 45 | 50 | 35 | 20 | 15 | 10 | 40 | 30 |
| | 1 | 5 | 9 | 10 | 7 | 4 | 3 | 2 | 8 | 6 |
| | 9 | 45 | 81 | 90 | 63 | 36 | 27 | 18 | 72 | 54 |
| | 4 | 20 | 36 | 40 | 28 | 16 | 12 | 8 | 32 | 24 |
| | 7 | 35 | 63 | 70 | 49 | 28 | 21 | 14 | 56 | 42 |
| | 3 | 15 | 27 | 30 | 21 | 12 | 9 | 6 | 24 | 18 |

**B**

| × | | | | | | | | | | |
|---|---|---|---|---|---|---|---|---|---|---|
| | 27 | 6 | 24 | 21 | 18 | 15 | 12 | 9 | 3 | |
| | 36 | 8 | 32 | 28 | 24 | | 16 | 12 | 4 | 40 |
| | 9 | 2 | 8 | 7 | 6 | 5 | 4 | 3 | 1 | 10 |
| | 18 | 4 | 16 | 14 | | 10 | 8 | 6 | 2 | 20 |
| | | 14 | 56 | 49 | 42 | | 28 | 21 | 7 | |
| | 72 | | 64 | 56 | 48 | 40 | 32 | 24 | 8 | 80 |
| | 45 | 10 | 40 | | 30 | 25 | 20 | 15 | 5 | |
| | 54 | 12 | 48 | 42 | 36 | 30 | 24 | 18 | 6 | 60 |
| | 90 | | 80 | 70 | 60 | | 40 | 30 | 10 | 100 |
| | 81 | 18 | 72 | | | 54 | 45 | 36 | 27 | 9 |

**C**

| × | | | | | | | | | | |
|---|---|---|---|---|---|---|---|---|---|---|
| | 100 | | 20 | | 70 | 50 | | 90 | | 10 |
| | 50 | 15 | | 20 | 35 | | 30 | | 40 | 5 |
| | 10 | 3 | | 4 | 7 | | 6 | 9 | | 1 |
| | | 9 | | 12 | 21 | 15 | | 27 | 24 | |
| | | 6 | 4 | 8 | | | 12 | 18 | 16 | 2 |
| | | 12 | 8 | 16 | 28 | 20 | | | 36 | 32 |
| | 90 | 27 | 18 | 36 | 63 | 45 | 54 | | 72 | |
| | | 18 | 12 | 24 | | 30 | 36 | 54 | 48 | 6 |
| | | 21 | | 28 | 49 | | 42 | | 56 | 7 |
| | | 24 | | 32 | 56 | 40 | | 72 | 64 | 8 |

**D**

| × | | | | | | | | | | |
|---|---|---|---|---|---|---|---|---|---|---|
| | 48 | | 42 | 12 | 36 | | 18 | 6 | | 30 |
| | 56 | 28 | | 14 | | 70 | 21 | | 63 | 35 |
| | | | 70 | | 60 | | | 10 | | 50 |
| | | 20 | 35 | | 30 | | 15 | 5 | 45 | |
| | 32 | | | 8 | | 40 | | | 36 | |
| | 8 | 4 | | 2 | | | 3 | 1 | | 5 |
| | | 8 | 14 | | 12 | | 6 | | 18 | 10 |
| | 64 | | 56 | | 48 | 80 | 24 | 8 | | 40 |
| | 72 | 36 | | 18 | | | 27 | | 81 | |
| | 24 | | 21 | | 18 | 30 | | 3 | 27 | |

Building Fluency with 0s–10s

▶ **PATH to FLUENCY** **Dashes 13–16**

## Complete each Dash. Check your answers on page 125.

| Dash 13<br>6s and 8s<br>Multiplications | Dash 14<br>6s and 8s<br>Divisions | Dash 15<br>7s and 8s<br>Multiplications | Dash 16<br>7s and 8s<br>Divisions |
|---|---|---|---|
| a. 6 × 9 = _____ | a. 72 / 8 = _____ | a. 7 × 3 = _____ | a. 63 / 7 = _____ |
| b. 8 * 2 = _____ | b. 12 ÷ 6 = _____ | b. 8 * 5 = _____ | b. 80 ÷ 8 = _____ |
| c. 4 • 6 = _____ | c. 16 / 8 = _____ | c. 2 • 7 = _____ | c. 14 / 7 = _____ |
| d. 7 × 8 = _____ | d. 24 ÷ 6 = _____ | d. 1 × 8 = _____ | d. 16 ÷ 8 = _____ |
| e. 6 * 1 = _____ | e. 8 / 8 = _____ | e. 7 * 9 = _____ | e. 7 / 7 = _____ |
| f. 8 • 9 = _____ | f. 6 ÷ 6 = _____ | f. 8 • 4 = _____ | f. 48 ÷ 8 = _____ |
| g. 3 × 6 = _____ | g. 40 / 8 = _____ | g. 4 × 7 = _____ | g. 35 / 7 = _____ |
| h. 4 * 8 = _____ | h. 42 ÷ 6 = _____ | h. 7 * 8 = _____ | h. 32 ÷ 8 = _____ |
| i. 6 • 8 = _____ | i. 24 / 8 = _____ | i. 7 • 1 = _____ | i. 21 / 7 = _____ |
| j. 8 × 1 = _____ | j. 18 ÷ 6 = _____ | j. 8 × 2 = _____ | j. 8 ÷ 8 = _____ |
| k. 2 * 6 = _____ | k. 48 / 8 = _____ | k. 5 * 7 = _____ | k. 28 / 7 = _____ |
| l. 3 • 8 = _____ | l. 48 ÷ 6 = _____ | l. 9 • 8 = _____ | l. 40 ÷ 8 = _____ |
| m. 6 × 5 = _____ | m. 64 / 8 = _____ | m. 7 × 6 = _____ | m. 49 / 7 = _____ |
| n. 8 * 8 = _____ | n. 42 ÷ 6 = _____ | n. 8 * 3 = _____ | n. 72 ÷ 8 = _____ |
| o. 6 • 6 = _____ | o. 56 / 8 = _____ | o. 7 • 7 = _____ | o. 42 / 7 = _____ |
| p. 5 × 8 = _____ | p. 30 ÷ 6 = _____ | p. 8 × 8 = _____ | p. 24 ÷ 8 = _____ |
| q. 6 * 7 = _____ | q. 32 / 8 = _____ | q. 7 * 0 = _____ | q. 56 / 7 = _____ |
| r. 8 × 0 = _____ | r. 54 ÷ 6 = _____ | r. 6 • 8 = _____ | r. 64 ÷ 8 = _____ |
| s. 0 * 6 = _____ | s. 80 / 8 = _____ | s. 8 × 0 = _____ | s. 70 / 7 = _____ |
| t. 6 • 10 = _____ | t. 60 ÷ 6 = _____ | t. 7 * 10 = _____ | t. 56 ÷ 8 = _____ |

▶ **PATH to FLUENCY** **Dashes 17–20**

## Complete each Dash. Check your answers on page 125.

| **Dash 17**<br>**6s and 7s**<br>**Multiplications** | **Dash 18**<br>**6s and 7s**<br>**Divisions** | **Dash 19**<br>**6s, 7s, 8s**<br>**Multiplications** | **Dash 20**<br>**6s, 7s, 8s**<br>**Divisions** |
|---|---|---|---|
| a. $6 \times 6 =$ _____ | a. $70 / 7 =$ _____ | a. $7 \times 7 =$ _____ | a. $21 / 7 =$ _____ |
| b. $7 * 7 =$ _____ | b. $60 \div 6 =$ _____ | b. $6 \cdot 3 =$ _____ | b. $16 \div 8 =$ _____ |
| c. $3 \cdot 6 =$ _____ | c. $28 / 7 =$ _____ | c. $8 * 6 =$ _____ | c. $54 / 6 =$ _____ |
| d. $8 \times 7 =$ _____ | d. $30 \div 6 =$ _____ | d. $6 \times 6 =$ _____ | d. $48 \div 8 =$ _____ |
| e. $6 * 1 =$ _____ | e. $42 / 7 =$ _____ | e. $7 \cdot 6 =$ _____ | e. $64 / 8 =$ _____ |
| f. $7 \cdot 2 =$ _____ | f. $24 \div 6 =$ _____ | f. $4 * 7 =$ _____ | f. $42 \div 6 =$ _____ |
| g. $9 \times 6 =$ _____ | g. $35 / 7 =$ _____ | g. $9 \times 7 =$ _____ | g. $56 / 7 =$ _____ |
| h. $9 * 7 =$ _____ | h. $12 \div 6 =$ _____ | h. $6 \cdot 9 =$ _____ | h. $72 \div 8 =$ _____ |
| i. $6 \cdot 8 =$ _____ | i. $7 / 7 =$ _____ | i. $6 * 4 =$ _____ | i. $18 / 6 =$ _____ |
| j. $7 \times 3 =$ _____ | j. $36 \div 6 =$ _____ | j. $8 \times 8 =$ _____ | j. $28 / 7 =$ _____ |
| k. $7 * 6 =$ _____ | k. $21 / 7 =$ _____ | k. $7 \cdot 3 =$ _____ | k. $56 \div 8 =$ _____ |
| l. $1 \cdot 7 =$ _____ | l. $48 \div 6 =$ _____ | l. $8 * 7 =$ _____ | l. $30 / 6 =$ _____ |
| m. $6 \times 2 =$ _____ | m. $63 / 7 =$ _____ | m. $6 \times 7 =$ _____ | m. $63 \div 7 =$ _____ |
| n. $7 * 5 =$ _____ | n. $6 \div 6 =$ _____ | n. $3 \cdot 6 =$ _____ | n. $32 / 8 =$ _____ |
| o. $4 \cdot 6 =$ _____ | o. $56 / 7 =$ _____ | o. $2 * 7 =$ _____ | o. $48 \div 6 =$ _____ |
| p. $6 \times 7 =$ _____ | p. $18 \div 6 =$ _____ | p. $9 \times 8 =$ _____ | p. $49 / 7 =$ _____ |
| q. $6 * 5 =$ _____ | q. $49 / 7 =$ _____ | q. $5 \cdot 6 =$ _____ | q. $36 \div 6 =$ _____ |
| r. $7 \cdot 4 =$ _____ | r. $42 \div 6 =$ _____ | r. $7 * 8 =$ _____ | r. $24 \div 8 =$ _____ |
| s. $6 \times 10 =$ _____ | s. $14 / 7 =$ _____ | s. $3 \times 7 =$ _____ | s. $42 / 7 =$ _____ |
| t. $7 \times 10 =$ _____ | t. $54 \div 6 =$ _____ | t. $9 \cdot 6 =$ _____ | t. $24 \div 6 =$ _____ |

© Houghton Mifflin Harcourt Publishing Company

► **PATH to FLUENCY** Dashes 9B–12B

Complete each multiplication and division Dash.
Check your answers on page 126.

| Dash 9B<br>2s, 5s, 9s, 10s<br>Multiplications | Dash 10B<br>2s, 5s, 9s, 10s<br>Divisions | Dash 11B<br>0s, 1s, 3s, 4s<br>Multiplications | Dash 12B<br>1s, 3s, 4s<br>Divisions |
|---|---|---|---|
| a.  $6 \times 2 =$ _____ | a.  $18 / 2 =$ _____ | a.  $7 \times 1 =$ _____ | a.  $2 / 1 =$ _____ |
| b.  $9 \cdot 4 =$ _____ | b.  $25 \div 5 =$ _____ | b.  $0 \cdot 6 =$ _____ | b.  $28 \div 4 =$ _____ |
| c.  $8 * 5 =$ _____ | c.  $70 / 10 =$ _____ | c.  $4 * 4 =$ _____ | c.  $3 / 3 =$ _____ |
| d.  $1 \times 10 =$ _____ | d.  $54 \div 9 =$ _____ | d.  $7 \times 3 =$ _____ | d.  $1 \div 1 =$ _____ |
| e.  $2 \cdot 7 =$ _____ | e.  $50 / 5 =$ _____ | e.  $3 \cdot 1 =$ _____ | e.  $40 / 4 =$ _____ |
| f.  $9 * 9 =$ _____ | f.  $81 \div 9 =$ _____ | f.  $4 * 7 =$ _____ | f.  $21 \div 3 =$ _____ |
| g.  $5 \times 6 =$ _____ | g.  $8 / 2 =$ _____ | g.  $9 \times 0 =$ _____ | g.  $5 / 1 =$ _____ |
| h. $10 \cdot 4 =$ _____ | h.  $90 \div 10 =$ _____ | h.  $1 \cdot 1 =$ _____ | h.  $16 \div 4 =$ _____ |
| i.  $7 * 5 =$ _____ | i.  $35 / 5 =$ _____ | i.  $3 * 4 =$ _____ | i.  $15 / 3 =$ _____ |
| j.  $8 \times 2 =$ _____ | j.  $27 / 9 =$ _____ | j.  $4 \times 9 =$ _____ | j.  $6 / 1 =$ _____ |
| k. $10 \cdot 10 =$ _____ | k.  $2 \div 2 =$ _____ | k.  $8 \cdot 1 =$ _____ | k.  $12 \div 4 =$ _____ |
| l.  $5 * 3 =$ _____ | l.  $36 / 9 =$ _____ | l.  $3 * 3 =$ _____ | l.  $27 / 3 =$ _____ |
| m. $9 \times 7 =$ _____ | m. $45 \div 5 =$ _____ | m. $0 \times 4 =$ _____ | m.  $9 \div 1 =$ _____ |
| n.  $9 \cdot 2 =$ _____ | n.  $14 / 2 =$ _____ | n. $10 \cdot 3 =$ _____ | n.  $8 / 4 =$ _____ |
| o.  $5 * 5 =$ _____ | o.  $20 \div 10 =$ _____ | o.  $6 * 4 =$ _____ | o.  $12 \div 3 =$ _____ |
| p.  $6 \times 9 =$ _____ | p.  $9 / 9 =$ _____ | p.  $1 \times 4 =$ _____ | p.  $3 / 1 =$ _____ |
| q.  $5 \cdot 2 =$ _____ | q.  $20 \div 5 =$ _____ | q.  $3 \cdot 6 =$ _____ | q.  $36 \div 4 =$ _____ |
| r.  $9 * 5 =$ _____ | r.  $45 \div 9 =$ _____ | r.  $4 * 8 =$ _____ | r.  $6 \div 3 =$ _____ |
| s.  $8 \times 10 =$ _____ | s.  $5 / 5 =$ _____ | s.  $7 \times 0 =$ _____ | s.  $4 / 1 =$ _____ |
| t.  $5 \cdot 10 =$ _____ | t.  $4 \div 2 =$ _____ | t.  $5 \cdot 3 =$ _____ | t.  $4 \div 4 =$ _____ |

**Name** _____    **Date** _____

▶ PATH to FLUENCY **Dashes 9C–12C**

## Complete each Dash. Check your answers on page 126.

| Dash 9C<br>2s, 5 ,9s, 10s<br>Multiplications | Dash 10C<br>2s, 5, 9s, 10s<br>Divisions | Dash 11C<br>0s, 1s ,3s, 4s<br>Multiplications | Dash 12C<br>1s, 3s, 4s<br>Divisions |
|---|---|---|---|
| a. 5 × 8 = ___ | a. 36 ÷ 9 = ___ | a. 0 × 7 = ___ | a. 4 / 1 = ___ |
| b. 9 * 9 = ___ | b. 30 / 5 = ___ | b. 1 * 4 = ___ | b. 15 ÷ 3 = ___ |
| c. 10 • 7 = ___ | c. 18 ÷ 2 = ___ | c. 3 • 6 = ___ | c. 24 / 4 = ___ |
| d. 4 × 5 = ___ | d. 80 / 10 = ___ | d. 4 × 9 = ___ | d. 9 ÷ 1 = ___ |
| e. 5 * 5 = ___ | e. 40 ÷ 5 = ___ | e. 8 * 0 = ___ | e. 21 / 3 = ___ |
| f. 10 • 3 = ___ | f. 72 / 9 = ___ | f. 7 * 1 = ___ | f. 12 ÷ 4 = ___ |
| g. 1 × 5 = ___ | g. 6 ÷ 2 = ___ | g. 4 • 3 = ___ | g. 5 / 1 = ___ |
| h. 3 * 9 = ___ | h. 54 / 9 = ___ | h. 4 × 4 = ___ | h. 3 ÷ 3 = ___ |
| i. 9 • 6 = ___ | i. 25 ÷ 5 = ___ | i. 0 * 5 = ___ | i. 32 / 4 = ___ |
| j. 10 × 8 = ___ | j. 10 / 10 = ___ | j. 1 • 6 = ___ | j. 2 ÷ 1 = ___ |
| k. 2 * 9 = ___ | k. 45 ÷ 5 = ___ | k. 3 × 2 = ___ | k. 18 / 3 = ___ |
| l. 6 • 2 = ___ | l. 27 / 9 = ___ | l. 4 * 7 = ___ | l. 36 ÷ 4 = ___ |
| m. 6 × 10 = ___ | m. 14 ÷ 2 = ___ | m. 1 • 0 = ___ | m. 7 / 1 = ___ |
| n. 8 * 9 = ___ | n. 35 / 5 = ___ | n. 2 × 1 = ___ | n. 24 ÷ 3 = ___ |
| o. 8 • 2 = ___ | o. 90 ÷ 9 = ___ | o. 9 * 3 = ___ | o. 4 / 4 = ___ |
| p. 4 × 2 = ___ | p. 90 / 10 = ___ | p. 2 • 4 = ___ | p. 6 ÷ 1 = ___ |
| q. 10 * 5 = ___ | q. 63 ÷ 9 = ___ | q. 0 × 3 = ___ | q. 12 / 3 = ___ |
| r. 10 • 10 = ___ | r. 15 / 5 = ___ | r. 1 * 1 = ___ | r. 20 ÷ 4 = ___ |
| s. 9 × 6 = ___ | s. 50 ÷ 10 = ___ | s. 3 • 9 = ___ | s. 8 / 1 = ___ |
| t. 5 * 7 = ___ | t. 8 / 2 = ___ | t. 4 × 5 = ___ | t. 27 ÷ 3 = ___ |

© Houghton Mifflin Harcourt Publishing Company

► PATH to FLUENCY **Answers to Dashes 13–20**

**Use this sheet to check your answers to the Dashes on pages 121 and 122.**

| Dash 13 × | Dash 14 ÷ | Dash 15 × | Dash 16 ÷ | Dash 17 × | Dash 18 ÷ | Dash 19 × | Dash 20 ÷ |
|---|---|---|---|---|---|---|---|
| a. 54 | a. 9 | a. 21 | a. 9 | a. 36 | a. 10 | a. 49 | a. 3 |
| b. 16 | b. 2 | b. 40 | b. 10 | b. 49 | b. 10 | b. 18 | b. 2 |
| c. 24 | c. 2 | c. 14 | c. 2 | c. 18 | c. 4 | c. 48 | c. 9 |
| d. 56 | d. 4 | d. 8 | d. 2 | d. 56 | d. 5 | d. 36 | d. 6 |
| e. 6 | e. 1 | e. 63 | e. 1 | e. 6 | e. 6 | e. 42 | e. 8 |
| f. 72 | f. 1 | f. 32 | f. 6 | f. 14 | f. 4 | f. 28 | f. 7 |
| g. 18 | g. 5 | g. 28 | g. 5 | g. 54 | g. 5 | g. 63 | g. 8 |
| h. 32 | h. 7 | h. 56 | h. 4 | h. 63 | h. 2 | h. 54 | h. 9 |
| i. 48 | i. 3 | i. 7 | i. 3 | i. 48 | i. 1 | i. 24 | i. 3 |
| j. 8 | j. 3 | j. 16 | j. 1 | j. 21 | j. 6 | j. 64 | j. 4 |
| k. 12 | k. 6 | k. 35 | k. 4 | k. 42 | k. 3 | k. 21 | k. 7 |
| l. 24 | l. 8 | l. 72 | l. 5 | l. 7 | l. 8 | l. 56 | l. 5 |
| m. 30 | m. 8 | m. 42 | m. 7 | m. 12 | m. 9 | m. 42 | m. 9 |
| n. 64 | n. 7 | n. 24 | n. 9 | n. 35 | n. 1 | n. 18 | n. 4 |
| o. 36 | o. 7 | o. 49 | o. 6 | o. 24 | o. 8 | o. 14 | o. 8 |
| p. 40 | p. 5 | p. 64 | p. 3 | p. 42 | p. 3 | p. 72 | p. 7 |
| q. 42 | q. 4 | q. 0 | q. 8 | q. 30 | q. 7 | q. 30 | q. 6 |
| r. 0 | r. 9 | r. 48 | r. 8 | r. 28 | r. 7 | r. 56 | r. 3 |
| s. 0 | s. 10 | s. 0 | s. 10 | s. 60 | s. 2 | s. 21 | s. 6 |
| t. 60 | t. 10 | t. 70 | t. 7 | t. 70 | t. 9 | t. 54 | t. 4 |

Name _____ Date _____

► PATH to FLUENCY **Answers to Dashes 9B–12C**

## Use this sheet to check your answers to the Dashes on pages 123 and 124.

| Dash 9B ✕ | Dash 10B ÷ | Dash 11B ✕ | Dash 12B ÷ | Dash 9C ✕ | Dash 10C ÷ | Dash 11C ✕ | Dash 12C ÷ |
|---|---|---|---|---|---|---|---|
| a. 12 | a. 9 | a. 7 | a. 2 | a. 40 | a. 4 | a. 0 | a. 4 |
| b. 36 | b. 5 | b. 0 | b. 7 | b. 81 | b. 6 | b. 4 | b. 5 |
| c. 40 | c. 7 | c. 16 | c. 1 | c. 70 | c. 9 | c. 18 | c. 6 |
| d. 10 | d. 6 | d. 21 | d. 1 | d. 20 | d. 8 | d. 36 | d. 9 |
| e. 14 | e. 10 | e. 3 | e. 10 | e. 25 | e. 8 | e. 0 | e. 7 |
| f. 81 | f. 9 | f. 28 | f. 7 | f. 30 | f. 8 | f. 7 | f. 3 |
| g. 30 | g. 4 | g. 0 | g. 5 | g. 5 | g. 3 | g. 12 | g. 5 |
| h. 40 | h. 9 | h. 1 | h. 4 | h. 27 | h. 6 | h. 16 | h. 1 |
| i. 35 | i. 7 | i. 12 | i. 5 | i. 54 | i. 5 | i. 0 | i. 8 |
| j. 16 | j. 3 | j. 36 | j. 6 | j. 80 | j. 1 | j. 6 | j. 2 |
| k. 100 | k. 1 | k. 8 | k. 3 | k. 18 | k. 9 | k. 6 | k. 6 |
| l. 15 | l. 4 | l. 9 | l. 9 | l. 12 | l. 3 | l. 28 | l. 9 |
| m. 63 | m. 9 | m. 0 | m. 9 | m. 60 | m. 7 | m. 0 | m. 7 |
| n. 18 | n. 7 | n. 30 | n. 2 | n. 72 | n. 7 | n. 2 | n. 8 |
| o. 25 | o. 2 | o. 24 | o. 4 | o. 16 | o. 10 | o. 27 | o. 1 |
| p. 54 | p. 1 | p. 4 | p. 3 | p. 8 | p. 9 | p. 8 | p. 6 |
| q. 10 | q. 4 | q. 18 | q. 9 | q. 50 | q. 7 | q. 0 | q. 4 |
| r. 45 | r. 5 | r. 32 | r. 2 | r. 100 | r. 3 | r. 1 | r. 5 |
| s. 80 | s. 1 | s. 0 | s. 4 | s. 54 | s. 5 | s. 27 | s. 8 |
| t. 50 | t. 2 | t. 15 | t. 1 | t. 35 | t. 4 | t. 20 | t. 9 |

## ► Choose the Operation

**Write an equation and solve the problem.**

1. Ernie helped his mother work in the yard for 3 days. He earned $6 each day. How much did he earn in all?

   _____

2. Ernie helped his mother work in the yard for 3 days. He earned $6 the first day, $5 the second day, and $7 the third day. How much did he earn in all?

   _____

3. Troy had $18. He gave $6 to each of his brothers and had no money left. How many brothers does Troy have?

   _____

4. Troy gave $18 to his brothers. He gave $4 to Raj, $7 to Darnell, and the rest to Jai. How much money did Jai get?

   _____

5. Jinja has 4 cousins. Grant has 7 more cousins than Jinja. How many cousins does Grant have?

   _____

6. Jinja has 4 cousins. Grant has 7 times as many cousins as Jinja. How many cousins does Grant have?

   _____

7. Camille has 15 fewer books than Jane has. Camille has 12 books. How many does Jane have?

   _____

8. Camille has 4 more books than Jane has. Camille has 15 books. How many books does Jane have?

   _____

## ▶ Write an Equation

**Write an equation and solve the problem.**

*Show your work.*

9. Luke had a $5 bill. He spent $3 on a sandwich. How much change did he get?

_____

10. Ramona is putting tiles on the kitchen floor. She will lay 8 rows of tiles, with 7 tiles in each row. How many tiles will Ramona use?

_____

11. Josh earned As on 6 tests last year. Jenna earned As on 6 times as many tests. How many As did Jenna earn?

_____

12. Sophie bought a stuffed animal for $3 and a board game for $7. How much money did Sophie spend?

_____

13. The Duarte family has 15 pets. Each of the 3 Duarte children care for the same number of pets. How many pets does each child care for?

_____

14. Ahmed spent $9 on a CD. Zal paid $6 more for the same CD at a different store. How much did Zal spend on the CD?

_____

Equations and Word Problems

## ▶ Write the Question

**Write a question for the given information and solve.**

15. Anna read 383 pages this month. Chris read 416 pages.

    **Question:** _____

    **Solution:** _____

16. Marisol had 128 beads in her jewelry box. She gave away 56 of them.

    **Question:** _____

    **Solution:** _____

17. Louis put 72 marbles in 8 bags. He put the same number of marbles in each bag.

    **Question:** _____

    **Solution:** _____

18. Geoff planted 4 pots of seeds. He planted 6 seeds in each pot.

    **Question:** _____

    **Solution:** _____

19. Marly put 10 books on each of 5 shelves in the library.

    **Question:** _____

    **Solution:** _____

## ► Write the Problem

**Write a problem that can be solved using the given equation. Then solve.**

20. $9 \times 6 = \square$    Solution: _____

_____

_____

21. $324 - 176 = \square$    Solution: _____

_____

_____

22. $56 \div 7 = \square$    Solution: _____

_____

_____

23. $459 + 535 = \square$    Solution: _____

_____

_____

24. **Math Journal** Choose an operation. Write a word problem that involves that operation. Write an equation to solve your word problem.

## ► Use Order of Operations

This exercise involves subtraction and multiplication:

$$10 - 3 \times 2$$

1. What do you get if you subtract first and then multiply? _____

2. What do you get if you multiply first and then subtract? _____

To make sure everyone has the same answer to problems like this one, people have decided that multiplication and division will be done *before* addition and subtraction. The answer you found in question 2 is correct.

If you want to tell people to add or subtract first, you must use parentheses. Parentheses mean "Do this first." For example, if you want people to subtract first in the exercise above, write it like this:

$$(10 - 3) \times 2$$

**Find the answer.**

3. $5 + 4 \times 2 =$ _____

4. $(9 - 3) \times 6 =$ _____

5. $8 \div 2 + 2 =$ _____

6. $6 \times (8 - 1) =$ _____

**Rewrite each statement, using symbols and numbers instead of words.**

7. Add 4 and 3, and multiply the total by 8. _____

8. Multiply 3 by 8, and add 4 to the total. _____

▶ **What's the Error?**

Dear Math Students,

Today I found the answer to 6 + 3 x 2.
Here is how I found the answer.

6 + 3 x 2

9 x 2 = 18

Is my answer correct? If not, please correct my work and tell me what I did wrong.

Your friend,
Puzzled Penguin

9. Write an answer to the Puzzled Penguin.

_____

_____

_____

**Find the answer.**

10. $4 + 3 \times 5 =$ _____

11. $10 \div 2 + 3 =$ _____

12. $12 - 9 \div 3 =$ _____

13. $3 \times 5 - 2 =$ _____

14. $(4 + 3) \times 5 =$ _____

15. $10 \div (2 + 3) =$ _____

16. $(12 - 9) \div 3 =$ _____

17. $3 \times (5 - 2) =$ _____

Write First Step Questions for Two Step Problems

## ► Write First Step Questions

**Write the first step question and answer.**
**Then solve the problem.**

*Show your work.*

18. A roller coaster has 7 cars. Each car has 4 seats. If there were 3 empty seats, how many people were on the roller coaster?

_____

_____

19. Each week, Marta earns $10 babysitting. She always spends $3 and saves the rest. How much does she save in 8 weeks?

_____

_____

20. Abu bought 6 packs of stickers. Each pack had 8 stickers. Then Abu's friend gave him 10 more stickers. How many stickers does Abu have now?

_____

_____

21. Zoe made some snacks. She put 4 apple slices and 2 melon slices on each plate. She prepared 5 plates. How many slices of fruit did Zoe use in all?

_____

_____

22. Kyle ordered 8 pizzas for his party. Each pizza was cut into 8 slices. 48 of the slices were plain cheese, and the rest had mushrooms. How many slices of pizza had mushrooms?

_____

_____

## ► Write First Step Questions (continued)

**Write the first step question and answer.**
**Then solve the problem.**

*Show your work.*

23. Nadia counted 77 birds on the pond. 53 were ducks, and the rest were geese. Then the geese flew away in 4 equal flocks. How many geese were in each flock?

_____

_____

24. Kagami baked 86 blueberry muffins. Her sisters ate 5 of them. Kagami divided the remaining muffins equally among 9 plates. How many muffins did she put on each plate?

_____

_____

25. Lucia had 42 plums. Jorge had 12 more plums than Lucia. Jorge divided his plums equally among 6 people. How many plums did each person get?

_____

_____

26. On his way to school, Kevin counted 5 mountain bikes and 3 road bikes. How many wheels were on the bikes altogether?

_____

_____

27. Juana has 21 shirts. Leslie had 7 less shirts than Juana, but then she bought 4 more. How many shirts does Leslie have now?

_____

_____

# ► Make Sense of Two Step Word Problems

**Write an equation and solve the problem.**

*Show your work.*

1. Nine hens laid 6 eggs each. Five of the eggs broke. How many eggs are left?

_____

2. There are 8 houses on Jeremiah's street. Each house has 1 willow tree, 6 apple trees, and 2 olive trees. How many trees are on Jeremiah's street in all?

_____

3. Tim has 9 marbles. Ryan has 3 fewer marbles than Tim. Leslie has 5 more marbles than Ryan. How many marbles does Leslie have?

_____

4. Mr. Helms has 2 stables with 4 horses in each stable. Ms. Martinez has 4 more horses than Mr. Helms. How many horses does Ms. Martinez have?

_____

5. Angela had $4. She bought 2 pumpkins for $1 each. How much money does Angela have now?

_____

6. Ahmad had $40. He bought an action figure for $5 and a backpack for $14. How much money does Ahmad have left?

_____

## ▶ More Make Sense of Two Step Problems

**Write an equation and solve the problem.**

*Show your work.*

7. In the locker room, there are 8 rows of 9 lockers. All of the lockers were full in the morning, but in the afternoon 6 were empty. How many lockers were full in the afternoon?

_____

8. Anita received 3 postcards of zebras and 2 postcards of monkeys each month for 3 months. How many postcards is that?

_____

9. The library has 2 books about the desert and 8 books about the rainforest. The books were divided into groups of 2. How many groups are there?

_____

10. Each pack of pencils contains 8 pencils. Sahil bought 3 packs and divided them equally among 6 people. How many pencils did each person get?

_____

11. James bought four 8-ounce bottles of water for a hiking trip. He drank 28 ounces. How many ounces of water are left?

_____

12. Kaya has 20 photos of dogs and 30 photos of cats. She displayed an equal number of them on 10 posters for a fund raiser for an animal shelter. How many photos were on each poster?

_____

## ▶ Multiply with Multiples of 10

When a number of ones is multiplied by 10, the ones become tens.

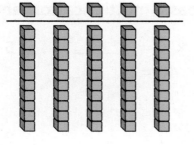

1 ten × 5 ones = 5 tens

$10 × 5 =$ _____

To multiply with multiples of 10, use place value and properties.

$2 × 3 = (2 × 1) × (3 × 1) = (2 × 3) × (1 × 1) = 6 × 1 = 6$

$2 × 30 = (2 × 1) × (3 × 10) = (2 × 3) × (1 × 10) = 6 × 10 = 60$

**Use a shortcut.**

Find the basic multiplication product. Then multiply by 10.

$$2 × 30$$
$$6 × 10 = 60$$

**Multiply.**

**1.** $6 × 40$

$× 10 =$ _____

**2.** $4 × 50$

$× 10 =$ _____

**3.** $70 × 8$

$× 10 =$ _____

**4.** $90 × 3$

$× 10 =$ _____

## ▶ Multiply Using Mental Math

**Use a basic multiplication and mental math to complete.**

5.  $3 \times 4 =$ _____
    $3 \times 40 =$ _____

6.  $1 \times 2 =$ _____
    $10 \times 2 =$ _____

7.  $9 \times 8 =$ _____
    $9 \times 80 =$ _____

8.  $2 \times 9 =$ _____
    $2 \times 90 =$ _____

9.  $5 \times 5 =$ _____
    $5 \times 50 =$ _____

10. $3 \times 5 =$ _____
    $3 \times 50 =$ _____

11. $1 \times 1 =$ _____
    $10 \times 1 =$ _____

12. $2 \times 3 =$ _____
    $20 \times 3 =$ _____

13. $5 \times 6 =$ _____
    $5 \times 60 =$ _____

14. $2 \times 4 =$ _____
    $2 \times 40 =$ _____

15. $6 \times 3 =$ _____
    $6 \times 30 =$ _____

16. $9 \times 2 =$ _____
    $9 \times 20 =$ _____

17. $2 \times 30 =$ _____

18. $5 \times 40 =$ _____

19. $9 \times 60 =$ _____

20. $3 \times 80 =$ _____

21. $2 \times 70 =$ _____

22. $5 \times 90 =$ _____

23. $9 \times 50 =$ _____

24. $5 \times 20 =$ _____

25. $3 \times 30 =$ _____

26. $5 \times 80 =$ _____

27. $9 \times 90 =$ _____

28. $5 \times 60 =$ _____

29. $70 \times 5 =$ _____

30. $8 \times 50 =$ _____

31. $60 \times 4 =$ _____

32. Describe how to multiply a one-digit number and
    a multiple of 10. _____

_____

► **PATH to FLUENCY** **Dashes 21–22, 19A–20A**

## Complete each Dash. Check your answers on page 143.

| Dash 21<br>2s, 3s, 4s, 5s, 9s<br>Multiplications | Dash 22<br>2s, 3s, 4s, 5s, 9s<br>Divisions | Dash 19A<br>6s, 7s, 8s<br>Multiplications | Dash 20A<br>6s, 7s, 8s<br>Divisions |
|---|---|---|---|
| a.  $6 \times 3 =$ _____ | a.  $16 / 4 =$ _____ | a.  $9 \times 6 =$ _____ | a.  $24 \div 6 =$ _____ |
| b.  $4 \cdot 7 =$ _____ | b.  $54 \div 9 =$ _____ | b.  $7 * 7 =$ _____ | b.  $21 / 7 =$ _____ |
| c.  $8 * 2 =$ _____ | c.  $4 / 2 =$ _____ | c.  $3 \cdot 7 =$ _____ | c.  $42 \div 7 =$ _____ |
| d.  $5 \times 3 =$ _____ | d.  $28 \div 4 =$ _____ | d.  $6 \times 3 =$ _____ | d.  $16 / 8 =$ _____ |
| e.  $4 \cdot 4 =$ _____ | e.  $25 / 5 =$ _____ | e.  $7 * 8 =$ _____ | e.  $24 \div 8 =$ _____ |
| f.  $3 \cdot 9 =$ _____ | f.  $21 \div 3 =$ _____ | f.  $8 \cdot 6 =$ _____ | f.  $54 / 6 =$ _____ |
| g.  $9 \times 9 =$ _____ | g.  $40 / 4 =$ _____ | g.  $5 \times 6 =$ _____ | g.  $36 \div 6 =$ _____ |
| h.  $8 \cdot 9 =$ _____ | h.  $81 \div 9 =$ _____ | h.  $6 * 6 =$ _____ | h.  $48 / 8 =$ _____ |
| i.  $6 * 4 =$ _____ | i.  $35 / 5 =$ _____ | i.  $9 \cdot 8 =$ _____ | i.  $49 \div 7 =$ _____ |
| j.  $3 \times 3 =$ _____ | j.  $12 / 3 =$ _____ | j.  $7 \times 6 =$ _____ | j.  $64 / 8 =$ _____ |
| k.  $2 \cdot 7 =$ _____ | k.  $2 \div 2 =$ _____ | k.  $2 * 7 =$ _____ | k.  $48 \div 6 =$ _____ |
| l.  $8 \cdot 5 =$ _____ | l.  $63 / 9 =$ _____ | l.  $4 \cdot 7 =$ _____ | l.  $42 / 6 =$ _____ |
| m.  $4 \times 9 =$ _____ | m.  $36 \div 4 =$ _____ | m.  $3 \times 6 =$ _____ | m.  $32 \div 8 =$ _____ |
| n.  $9 \cdot 5 =$ _____ | n.  $18 / 2 =$ _____ | n.  $9 * 7 =$ _____ | n.  $56 / 7 =$ _____ |
| o.  $7 * 3 =$ _____ | o.  $9 \div 3 =$ _____ | o.  $6 \cdot 7 =$ _____ | o.  $63 \div 7 =$ _____ |
| p.  $2 \times 2 =$ _____ | p.  $36 / 9 =$ _____ | p.  $6 \times 9 =$ _____ | p.  $72 / 8 =$ _____ |
| q.  $8 \cdot 4 =$ _____ | q.  $40 \div 5 =$ _____ | q.  $8 * 7 =$ _____ | q.  $30 \div 6 =$ _____ |
| r.  $5 * 1 =$ _____ | r.  $12 \div 4 =$ _____ | r.  $6 \cdot 4 =$ _____ | r.  $18 / 6 =$ _____ |
| s.  $5 \times 5 =$ _____ | s.  $9 / 9 =$ _____ | s.  $7 \times 3 =$ _____ | s.  $56 \div 8 =$ _____ |
| t.  $6 \cdot 9 =$ _____ | t.  $14 \div 2 =$ _____ | t.  $8 * 8 =$ _____ | t.  $28 / 7 =$ _____ |

► PATH to FLUENCY Dashes 21A–22A, 19B–20B

## Complete each Dash. Check your answers on page 143.

| Dash 21A<br>2s, 3s, 4s, 5s, 9s<br>Multiplications | Dash 22A<br>2s, 3s, 4s, 5s, 9s<br>Divisions | Dash 19B<br>6s, 7s, 8s<br>Multiplications | Dash 20B<br>6s, 7s, 8s<br>Divisions |
|---|---|---|---|
| a. $6 \times 9 =$ _____ | a. $14 \div 2 =$ _____ | a. $6 \times 2 =$ _____ | a. $36 \div 6 =$ _____ |
| b. $6 * 3 =$ _____ | b. $16 / 4 =$ _____ | b. $7 * 7 =$ _____ | b. $63 / 7 =$ _____ |
| c. $4 \cdot 7 =$ _____ | c. $9 \div 9 =$ _____ | c. $8 \cdot 5 =$ _____ | c. $24 \div 8 =$ _____ |
| d. $5 \times 5 =$ _____ | d. $54 / 9 =$ _____ | d. $4 \times 6 =$ _____ | d. $18 / 6 =$ _____ |
| e. $8 * 2 =$ _____ | e. $12 \div 4 =$ _____ | e. $3 * 7 =$ _____ | e. $28 \div 7 =$ _____ |
| f. $5 \cdot 1 =$ _____ | f. $4 / 2 =$ _____ | f. $1 \cdot 8 =$ _____ | f. $48 / 8 =$ _____ |
| g. $5 \times 3 =$ _____ | g. $40 \div 5 =$ _____ | g. $6 \times 9 =$ _____ | g. $54 \div 6 =$ _____ |
| h. $8 * 4 =$ _____ | h. $28 / 4 =$ _____ | h. $7 * 5 =$ _____ | h. $42 / 7 =$ _____ |
| i. $4 \cdot 4 =$ _____ | i. $36 \div 9 =$ _____ | i. $8 \cdot 3 =$ _____ | i. $72 \div 8 =$ _____ |
| j. $2 \times 2 =$ _____ | j. $25 / 5 =$ _____ | j. $4 \times 6 =$ _____ | j. $6 / 6 =$ _____ |
| k. $3 * 9 =$ _____ | k. $9 \div 3 =$ _____ | k. $9 * 7 =$ _____ | k. $14 \div 7 =$ _____ |
| l. $7 \cdot 3 =$ _____ | l. $21 / 3 =$ _____ | l. $8 \cdot 8 =$ _____ | l. $56 / 8 =$ _____ |
| m. $9 \times 9 =$ _____ | m. $18 \div 2 =$ _____ | m. $6 \times 1 =$ _____ | m. $12 \div 6 =$ _____ |
| n. $9 * 5 =$ _____ | n. $40 / 4 =$ _____ | n. $7 * 4 =$ _____ | n. $7 / 7 =$ _____ |
| o. $8 \cdot 9 =$ _____ | o. $36 \div 4 =$ _____ | o. $8 \cdot 6 =$ _____ | o. $16 \div 8 =$ _____ |
| p. $4 \times 9 =$ _____ | p. $81 / 9 =$ _____ | p. $7 \times 6 =$ _____ | p. $30 / 6 =$ _____ |
| q. $6 * 4 =$ _____ | q. $63 \div 9 =$ _____ | q. $2 * 7 =$ _____ | q. $56 \div 7 =$ _____ |
| r. $8 \cdot 5 =$ _____ | r. $35 / 5 =$ _____ | r. $9 \cdot 8 =$ _____ | r. $8 / 8 =$ _____ |
| s. $2 \times 7 =$ _____ | s. $12 \div 3 =$ _____ | s. $6 \times 5 =$ _____ | s. $48 \div 6 =$ _____ |
| t. $3 * 3 =$ _____ | t. $2 / 2 =$ _____ | t. $7 * 6 =$ _____ | t. $21 / 7 =$ _____ |

© Houghton Mifflin Harcourt Publishing Company

► **PATH to FLUENCY** **Dashes 21B–22B, 19C–20C**

**Complete each Dash. Check your answers on page 144.**

| Dash 21B 2s, 3s, 4s, 5s, 9s Multiplications | Dash 22B 2s, 3s, 4s, 5s, 9s Divisions | Dash 19C 6s, 7s, 8s Multiplications | |
|---|---|---|---|
| a. $2 \times 3 =$ _____ | a. $8 \div 2 =$ _____ | a. $6 \times 8 =$ _____ | a. 54 |
| b. $3 * 8 =$ _____ | b. $18 / 3 =$ _____ | b. $7 * 3 =$ _____ | b. 49 |
| c. $4 \cdot 4 =$ _____ | c. $12 \div 4 =$ _____ | c. $8 \cdot 6 =$ _____ | c. 24 |
| d. $5 \times 6 =$ _____ | d. $25 / 5 =$ _____ | d. $2 \times 6 =$ _____ | d. 6 / |
| e. $9 * 8 =$ _____ | e. $63 \div 9 =$ _____ | e. $8 * 7 =$ _____ | e. 35 ÷ |
| f. $9 \cdot 2 =$ _____ | f. $16 / 2 =$ _____ | f. $9 \cdot 8 =$ _____ | f. 72 / |
| g. $3 \times 3 =$ _____ | g. $3 \div 3 =$ _____ | g. $6 \times 4 =$ _____ | g. $18 \div 6 =$ |
| h. $4 * 2 =$ _____ | h. $28 / 4 =$ _____ | h. $7 * 1 =$ _____ | h. $28 / 7 =$ _____ |
| i. $9 \cdot 5 =$ _____ | i. $45 \div 5 =$ _____ | i. $8 \cdot 3 =$ _____ | i. $8 \div 8 =$ _____ |
| j. $9 \times 4 =$ _____ | j. $27 / 9 =$ _____ | j. $5 \times 6 =$ _____ | j. $30 / 6 =$ _____ |
| k. $2 * 7 =$ _____ | k. $12 \div 2 =$ _____ | k. $9 * 7 =$ _____ | k. $21 \div 7 =$ _____ |
| l. $3 \cdot 5 =$ _____ | l. $12 / 3 =$ _____ | l. $4 \cdot 8 =$ _____ | l. $40 / 8 =$ _____ |
| m. $4 \times 8 =$ _____ | m. $20 \div 4 =$ _____ | m. $6 \times 6 =$ _____ | m. $42 \div 6 =$ _____ |
| n. $5 * 3 =$ _____ | n. $40 / 5 =$ _____ | n. $7 * 5 =$ _____ | n. $63 / 7 =$ _____ |
| o. $9 \cdot 6 =$ _____ | o. $54 \div 9 =$ _____ | o. $8 \cdot 8 =$ _____ | o. $32 \div 8 =$ _____ |
| p. $2 \times 8 =$ _____ | p. $2 / 2 =$ _____ | p. $1 \times 6 =$ _____ | p. $36 / 6 =$ _____ |
| q. $3 * 7 =$ _____ | q. $9 \div 3 =$ _____ | q. $2 * 7 =$ _____ | q. $14 \div 7 =$ _____ |
| r. $4 \cdot 1 =$ _____ | r. $36 / 4 =$ _____ | r. $5 \cdot 8 =$ _____ | r. $56 / 8 =$ _____ |
| s. $5 \times 8 =$ _____ | s. $15 \div 5 =$ _____ | s. $6 \times 9 =$ _____ | s. $24 \div 6 =$ _____ |
| t. $9 * 9 =$ _____ | t. $9 / 9 =$ _____ | t. $7 * 7 =$ _____ | t. $42 / 7 =$ _____ |

Name _____ Date _____

# Dashes 21C–22C, 19D–20D

▶ each Dash. Check your answers on page 144.

| h 21C 4s, 5s, 9s plications | Dash 22C 2s, 3s, 4s, 5s, 9s Divisions | Dash 19D 6s, 7s, 8s Multiplications | Dash 20D 6s, 7s, 8s Divisions |
|---|---|---|---|
| × 9 = _____ | a. 8 ÷ 2 = _____ | a. 6 × 9 = _____ | a. 18 / 6 = _____ |
| * 7 = _____ | b. 6 / 3 = _____ | b. 7 * 6 = _____ | b. 42 ÷ 7 = _____ |
| 4 • 5 = _____ | c. 4 ÷ 4 = _____ | c. 8 • 2 = _____ | c. 32 / 8 = _____ |
| 5 × 3 = _____ | d. 20 / 5 = _____ | d. 3 × 6 = _____ | d. 54 ÷ 6 = _____ |
| 9 * 1 = _____ | e. 63 ÷ 9 = _____ | e. 4 * 7 = _____ | e. 49 / 7 = _____ |
| f. 1 • 2 = _____ | f. 16 / 2 = _____ | f. 9 • 8 = _____ | f. 8 / 8 = _____ |
| g. 4 × 3 = _____ | g. 15 ÷ 3 = _____ | g. 6 × 6 = _____ | g. 30 ÷ 6 = _____ |
| h. 4 * 1 = _____ | h. 32 / 4 = _____ | h. 7 * 2 = _____ | h. 35 / 7 = _____ |
| i. 7 • 5 = _____ | i. 30 ÷ 5 = _____ | i. 8 • 1 = _____ | i. 48 ÷ 8 = _____ |
| j. 9 × 9 = _____ | j. 45 / 9 = _____ | j. 2 × 6 = _____ | j. 24 / 6 = _____ |
| k. 2 * 3 = _____ | k. 2 ÷ 2 = _____ | k. 8 * 7 = _____ | k. 14 ÷ 7 = _____ |
| l. 3 • 8 = _____ | l. 21 / 3 = _____ | l. 3 • 8 = _____ | l. 56 / 8 = _____ |
| m. 4 × 4 = _____ | m. 12 ÷ 4 = _____ | m. 6 × 4 = _____ | m. 6 ÷ 6 = _____ |
| n. 5 * 2 = _____ | n. 10 / 5 = _____ | n. 7 * 5 = _____ | n. 21 / 7 = _____ |
| o. 9 • 6 = _____ | o. 9 ÷ 9 = _____ | o. 8 • 8 = _____ | o. 40 ÷ 8 = _____ |
| p. 6 × 2 = _____ | p. 12 / 2 = _____ | p. 1 × 6 = _____ | p. 48 / 6 = _____ |
| q. 9 * 3 = _____ | q. 27 ÷ 3 = _____ | q. 3 * 7 = _____ | q. 56 ÷ 7 = _____ |
| r. 6 • 4 = _____ | r. 20 / 4 = _____ | r. 4 • 8 = _____ | r. 64 / 8 = _____ |
| s. 5 × 5 = _____ | s. 40 ÷ 8 = _____ | s. 6 × 7 = _____ | s. 36 ÷ 6 = _____ |
| t. 3 * 9 = _____ | t. 81 / 9 = _____ | t. 7 * 7 = _____ | t. 7 / 7 = _____ |

## ► Answers to Dashes 21–22, 19A–20B, 21A–22A

**Use this sheet to check your answers to the Dashes on pages 139 and 140.**

| Dash 21 × | Dash 22 ÷ | Dash 19A × | Dash 20A ÷ | Dash 21A × | Dash 22A ÷ | Dash 19B × | Dash 20B ÷ |
|---|---|---|---|---|---|---|---|
| a. 18 | a. 4 | a. 54 | a. 4 | a. 54 | a. 7 | a. 12 | a. 6 |
| b. 28 | b. 6 | b. 49 | b. 3 | b. 18 | b. 4 | b. 49 | b. 9 |
| c. 16 | c. 2 | c. 21 | c. 6 | c. 28 | c. 1 | c. 40 | c. 3 |
| d. 15 | d. 7 | d. 18 | d. 2 | d. 25 | d. 6 | d. 24 | d. 3 |
| e. 16 | e. 5 | e. 56 | e. 3 | e. 16 | e. 3 | e. 21 | e. 4 |
| f. 27 | f. 7 | f. 48 | f. 9 | f. 5 | f. 2 | f. 8 | f. 6 |
| g. 81 | g. 10 | g. 30 | g. 6 | g. 15 | g. 8 | g. 54 | g. 9 |
| h. 72 | h. 9 | h. 36 | h. 6 | h. 32 | h. 7 | h. 35 | h. 6 |
| i. 24 | i. 7 | i. 72 | i. 7 | i. 16 | i. 4 | i. 24 | i. 9 |
| j. 9 | j. 4 | j. 42 | j. 8 | j. 4 | j. 5 | j. 24 | j. 1 |
| k. 14 | k. 1 | k. 14 | k. 8 | k. 27 | k. 3 | k. 63 | k. 2 |
| l. 40 | l. 7 | l. 28 | l. 7 | l. 21 | l. 7 | l. 64 | l. 7 |
| m. 36 | m. 9 | m. 18 | m. 4 | m. 81 | m. 9 | m. 6 | m. 2 |
| n. 45 | n. 9 | n. 63 | n. 8 | n. 45 | n. 10 | n. 28 | n. 1 |
| o. 21 | o. 3 | o. 42 | o. 9 | o. 72 | o. 9 | o. 48 | o. 2 |
| p. 4 | p. 4 | p. 54 | p. 9 | p. 36 | p. 9 | p. 42 | p. 5 |
| q. 32 | q. 8 | q. 56 | q. 5 | q. 24 | q. 7 | q. 14 | q. 8 |
| r. 5 | r. 3 | r. 24 | r. 3 | r. 40 | r. 7 | r. 72 | r. 1 |
| s. 25 | s. 1 | s. 21 | s. 7 | s. 14 | s. 4 | s. 30 | s. 8 |
| t. 54 | t. 7 | t. 64 | t. 4 | t. 9 | t. 1 | t. 42 | t. 3 |

# ► Answers to Dashes 21B–22B, 19C–22C, 19D, 20D

## Use this sheet to check your answers to the Dashes on pages 141 and 142.

| Dash 21B × | Dash 22B ÷ | Dash 19C × | Dash 20C ÷ | Dash 21C × | Dash 22C ÷ | Dash 19D × | Dash 20D ÷ |
|---|---|---|---|---|---|---|---|
| a. 6 | a. 4 | a. 48 | a. 9 | a. 18 | a. 4 | a. 54 | a. 3 |
| b. 24 | b. 6 | b. 21 | b. 7 | b. 21 | b. 2 | b. 42 | b. 6 |
| c. 16 | c. 3 | c. 48 | c. 3 | c. 20 | c. 1 | c. 16 | c. 4 |
| d. 30 | d. 5 | d. 12 | d. 1 | d. 15 | d. 4 | d. 18 | d. 9 |
| e. 72 | e. 7 | e. 56 | e. 5 | e. 9 | e. 7 | e. 28 | e. 7 |
| f. 18 | f. 8 | f. 72 | f. 9 | f. 2 | f. 8 | f. 72 | f. 1 |
| g. 9 | g. 1 | g. 24 | g. 3 | g. 12 | g. 5 | g. 36 | g. 5 |
| h. 8 | h. 7 | h. 7 | h. 4 | h. 4 | h. 8 | h. 14 | h. 5 |
| i. 45 | i. 9 | i. 24 | i. 1 | i. 35 | i. 6 | i. 8 | i. 6 |
| j. 36 | j. 3 | j. 30 | j. 5 | j. 81 | j. 5 | j. 12 | j. 4 |
| k. 14 | k. 6 | k. 63 | k. 3 | k. 6 | k. 1 | k. 56 | k. 2 |
| l. 15 | l. 4 | l. 32 | l. 5 | l. 24 | l. 7 | l. 24 | l. 7 |
| m. 32 | m. 5 | m. 36 | m. 7 | m. 16 | m. 3 | m. 24 | m. 1 |
| n. 15 | n. 8 | n. 35 | n. 9 | n. 10 | n. 2 | n. 35 | n. 3 |
| o. 54 | o. 6 | o. 64 | o. 4 | o. 54 | o. 1 | o. 64 | o. 5 |
| p. 16 | p. 1 | p. 6 | p. 6 | p. 12 | p. 6 | p. 6 | p. 8 |
| q. 21 | q. 3 | q. 14 | q. 2 | q. 27 | q. 9 | q. 21 | q. 8 |
| r. 4 | r. 9 | r. 40 | r. 7 | r. 24 | r. 5 | r. 32 | r. 8 |
| s. 40 | s. 3 | s. 54 | s. 4 | s. 25 | s. 5 | s. 42 | s. 6 |
| t. 81 | t. 1 | t. 49 | t. 6 | t. 27 | t. 9 | t. 49 | t. 1 |

## ▶ Solve Two Step Word Problems

**Write an equation and solve the problem.**

*Show your work.*

1. Raul spent 10 minutes doing homework for each of 5 subjects and 15 minutes for another subject. How many minutes did Raul spend on his homework?

   _____

2. At Sonya's cello recital, there were 8 rows of chairs, with 6 chairs in each row. There was a person in each chair, and there were 17 more people standing. How many people were in the audience altogether?

   _____

3. Jana played a game with a deck of cards. She placed the cards on the floor in 3 rows of 10. If the deck has 52 cards, how many cards did Jana leave out?

   _____

4. Mukesh was making 7 salads. He opened a can of olives and put 6 olives on each salad. Then he ate the rest of the olives in the can. If there were 51 olives to start with, how many olives did Mukesh eat?

   _____

5. Peter wallpapered a wall that was 8 feet wide and 9 feet high. He had 28 square feet of wallpaper left over. How many square feet of wallpaper did he start with?

   _____

► PATH to FLUENCY **What's My Rule?**

A **function table** is a table of ordered pairs. For every input number, there is only one output number. The rule describes what to do to the input number to get the output number.

**Write the rule and then complete the function table.**

6. **Rule:** _____

| Input | Output |
|-------|--------|
| 7 | 42 |
| 8 | _____ |
| _____ | 54 |
| 6 | 36 |

7. **Rule:** _____

| Input | Output |
|-------|--------|
| 81 | 9 |
| 45 | 5 |
| 72 | _____ |
| _____ | 7 |

8. **Rule:** _____

| Input | Output |
|-------|--------|
| 4 | 28 |
| 8 | 56 |
| 6 | _____ |
| 7 | _____ |

9. **Rule:** _____

| Input | Output |
|-------|--------|
| 32 | 8 |
| 8 | 2 |
| _____ | 3 |
| 24 | _____ |

10. **Rule:** _____

| Input | Output |
|-------|--------|
| 21 | 7 |
| 27 | 9 |
| _____ | 6 |
| 15 | _____ |

11. **Rule:** _____

| Input | Output |
|-------|--------|
| 5 | 25 |
| _____ | 40 |
| 9 | _____ |
| 3 | 15 |

► PATH to FLUENCY **Play *Division Three-in-a-Row***

**Rules for *Division Three-in-a-Row***

*Number of players:* 2
*What You Will Need:* Division Product Cards, one
*Three-in-a-Row* Game Grid for each player

1. Each player writes any nine quotients in the squares
   of a game grid. A player may write the same
   quotient more than once.

2. Shuffle the cards. Place them division side up in a
   stack in the center of the table.

3. Players take turns. On each turn, a player
   completes the division on the top card and then
   partners check the answer.

4. For a correct answer, if the quotient is on the game
   grid, the player puts an X through that grid square.
   If the answer is wrong, or if the quotient is not on
   the grid, the player doesn't mark anything. The
   player puts the card division side up on the bottom
   of the stack.

5. The first player to mark three squares in a row
   (horizontally, vertically, or diagonally) wins.

*Three-in-a-Row* Game Grids

$2 \times 2$

$2 \cdot 3$

Hint:
What is $3 \cdot 2$?
© Houghton Mifflin Harcourt Publishing Company

$2 * 4$

Hint:
What is $4 * 2$?
© Houghton Mifflin Harcourt Publishing Company

$2 \times 5$

Hint:
What is $5 \times 2$?
© Houghton Mifflin Harcourt Publishing Company

$2 \times 6$

Hint:
What is $6 \times 2$?
© Houghton Mifflin Harcourt Publishing Company

$2 \cdot 7$

Hint:
What is $7 \cdot 2$?
© Houghton Mifflin Harcourt Publishing Company

$2 * 8$

Hint:
What is $8 * 2$?
© Houghton Mifflin Harcourt Publishing Company

$2 \times 9$

Hint:
What is $9 \times 2$?
© Houghton Mifflin Harcourt Publishing Company

$5 \times 2$

Hint:
What is $2 \times 5$?
© Houghton Mifflin Harcourt Publishing Company

$5 \cdot 3$

Hint:
What is $3 \cdot 5$?
© Houghton Mifflin Harcourt Publishing Company

$5 * 4$

Hint:
What is $4 * 5$?
© Houghton Mifflin Harcourt Publishing Company

$5 \times 5$

© Houghton Mifflin Harcourt Publishing Company

$5 \times 6$

Hint:
What is $6 \times 5$?
© Houghton Mifflin Harcourt Publishing Company

$5 \cdot 7$

Hint:
What is $7 \cdot 5$?
© Houghton Mifflin Harcourt Publishing Company

$5 * 8$

Hint:
What is $8 * 5$?
© Houghton Mifflin Harcourt Publishing Company

$5 \times 9$

Hint:
What is $9 \times 5$?
© Houghton Mifflin Harcourt Publishing Company

© Houghton Mifflin Harcourt Publishing Company

**Name** _____  **Date** _____

$2\overline{)10}$

Hint: What is
$\square \times 2 = 10$?
© Houghton Mifflin Harcourt Publishing Company

$2\overline{)8}$

Hint: What is
$\square \times 2 = 8$?
© Houghton Mifflin Harcourt Publishing Company

$2\overline{)6}$

Hint: What is
$\square \times 2 = 6$?
© Houghton Mifflin Harcourt Publishing Company

$2\overline{)4}$

Hint: What is
$\square \times 2 = 4$?
© Houghton Mifflin Harcourt Publishing Company

$2\overline{)18}$

Hint: What is
$\square \times 2 = 18$?
© Houghton Mifflin Harcourt Publishing Company

$2\overline{)16}$

Hint: What is
$\square \times 2 = 16$?
© Houghton Mifflin Harcourt Publishing Company

$2\overline{)14}$

Hint: What is
$\square \times 2 = 14$?
© Houghton Mifflin Harcourt Publishing Company

$2\overline{)12}$

Hint: What is
$\square \times 2 = 12$?
© Houghton Mifflin Harcourt Publishing Company

$5\overline{)25}$

Hint: What is
$\square \times 5 = 25$?
© Houghton Mifflin Harcourt Publishing Company

$5\overline{)20}$

Hint: What is
$\square \times 5 = 20$?
© Houghton Mifflin Harcourt Publishing Company

$5\overline{)15}$

Hint: What is
$\square \times 5 = 15$?
© Houghton Mifflin Harcourt Publishing Company

$5\overline{)10}$

Hint: What is
$\square \times 5 = 10$?
© Houghton Mifflin Harcourt Publishing Company

$5\overline{)45}$

Hint: What is
$\square \times 5 = 45$?
© Houghton Mifflin Harcourt Publishing Company

$5\overline{)40}$

Hint: What is
$\square \times 5 = 40$?
© Houghton Mifflin Harcourt Publishing Company

$5\overline{)35}$

Hint: What is
$\square \times 5 = 35$?
© Houghton Mifflin Harcourt Publishing Company

$5\overline{)30}$

Hint: What is
$\square \times 5 = 30$?
© Houghton Mifflin Harcourt Publishing Company

Product Cards: 2s, 5s, 9s

$9 \times 2$

Hint:
What is $2 \times 9$?

$9 \cdot 3$

Hint:
What is $3 \cdot 9$?

$9 * 4$

Hint:
What is $4 * 9$?

$9 \times 5$

Hint:
What is $5 \times 9$?

$9 \times 6$

Hint:
What is $6 \times 9$?

$9 \cdot 7$

Hint:
What is $7 \cdot 9$?

$9 * 8$

Hint:
What is $8 * 9$?

$9 \times 9$

$\times$

$\bullet$

$*$

$\times$

$\times$

$\bullet$

$*$

$\times$

You can write any numbers on the last 8 cards. Use them to practice difficult problems or if you lose a card.

**Name** _____

**Date** _____

$9\overline{)45}$

Hint: What is
$\square \times 9 = 45$?
© Houghton Mifflin Harcourt Publishing Company

$9\overline{)36}$

Hint: What is
$\square \times 9 = 36$?
© Houghton Mifflin Harcourt Publishing Company

$9\overline{)27}$

Hint: What is
$\square \times 9 = 27$?
© Houghton Mifflin Harcourt Publishing Company

$9\overline{)18}$

Hint: What is
$\square \times 9 = 18$?
© Houghton Mifflin Harcourt Publishing Company

$9\overline{)81}$

Hint: What is
$\square \times 9 = 81$?
© Houghton Mifflin Harcourt Publishing Company

$9\overline{)72}$

Hint: What is
$\square \times 9 = 72$?
© Houghton Mifflin Harcourt Publishing Company

$9\overline{)63}$

Hint: What is
$\square \times 9 = 63$?
© Houghton Mifflin Harcourt Publishing Company

$9\overline{)54}$

Hint: What is
$\square \times 9 = 54$?
© Houghton Mifflin Harcourt Publishing Company

You can write any numbers on the last 8 cards. Use them to practice difficult problems or if you lose a card.

Product Cards: 2s, 5s, 9s

**Class Activity**

**Name**

**Date**

$3 \times 2$

Hint:
What is $2 \times 3$?

$3 \cdot 3$

$3 * 4$

Hint:
What is $4 * 3$?

$3 \times 5$

Hint:
What is $5 \times 3$?

$3 \times 6$

Hint:
What is $6 \times 3$?

$3 \cdot 7$

Hint:
What is $7 \cdot 3$?

$3 * 8$

Hint:
What is $8 * 3$?

$3 \times 9$

Hint:
What is $9 \times 3$?

$4 \times 2$

Hint:
What is $2 \times 4$?

$4 \cdot 3$

Hint:
What is $3 \cdot 4$?

$4 * 4$

$4 \times 5$

Hint:
What is $5 \times 4$?

$4 \times 6$

Hint:
What is $6 \times 4$?

$4 \cdot 7$

Hint:
What is $7 \cdot 4$?

$4 * 8$

Hint:
What is $8 * 4$?

$4 \times 9$

Hint:
What is $9 \times 4$?

Product Cards: 3s, 4s **149E**

$3\overline{)15}$

Hint: What is

$\square \times 3 = 15?$

© Houghton Mifflin Harcourt Publishing Company

$3\overline{)12}$

Hint: What is

$\square \times 3 = 12?$

© Houghton Mifflin Harcourt Publishing Company

$3\overline{)9}$

Hint: What is

$\square \times 3 = 9?$

© Houghton Mifflin Harcourt Publishing Company

$3\overline{)6}$

Hint: What is

$\square \times 3 = 6?$

© Houghton Mifflin Harcourt Publishing Company

$3\overline{)27}$

Hint: What is

$\square \times 3 = 27?$

© Houghton Mifflin Harcourt Publishing Company

$3\overline{)24}$

Hint: What is

$\square \times 3 = 24?$

© Houghton Mifflin Harcourt Publishing Company

$3\overline{)21}$

Hint: What is

$\square \times 3 = 21?$

© Houghton Mifflin Harcourt Publishing Company

$3\overline{)18}$

Hint: What is

$\square \times 3 = 18?$

© Houghton Mifflin Harcourt Publishing Company

$4\overline{)20}$

Hint: What is

$\square \times 4 = 20?$

© Houghton Mifflin Harcourt Publishing Company

$4\overline{)16}$

Hint: What is

$\square \times 4 = 16?$

© Houghton Mifflin Harcourt Publishing Company

$4\overline{)12}$

Hint: What is

$\square \times 4 = 12?$

© Houghton Mifflin Harcourt Publishing Company

$4\overline{)8}$

Hint: What is

$\square \times 4 = 8?$

© Houghton Mifflin Harcourt Publishing Company

$4\overline{)36}$

Hint: What is

$\square \times 4 = 36?$

© Houghton Mifflin Harcourt Publishing Company

$4\overline{)32}$

Hint: What is

$\square \times 4 = 32?$

© Houghton Mifflin Harcourt Publishing Company

$4\overline{)28}$

Hint: What is

$\square \times 4 = 28?$

© Houghton Mifflin Harcourt Publishing Company

$4\overline{)24}$

Hint: What is

$\square \times 4 = 24?$

© Houghton Mifflin Harcourt Publishing Company

© Houghton Mifflin Harcourt Publishing Company

$6 \times 2$

Hint:
What is $2 \times 6$?
© Houghton Mifflin Harcourt Publishing Company

$6 \cdot 3$

Hint:
What is $3 \cdot 6$?
© Houghton Mifflin Harcourt Publishing Company

$6 * 4$

Hint:
What is $4 * 6$?
© Houghton Mifflin Harcourt Publishing Company

$6 \times 5$

Hint:
What is $5 \times 6$?
© Houghton Mifflin Harcourt Publishing Company

$6 \times 6$

© Houghton Mifflin Harcourt Publishing Company

$6 \cdot 7$

Hint:
What is $7 \cdot 6$?
© Houghton Mifflin Harcourt Publishing Company

$6 * 8$

Hint:
What is $8 * 6$?
© Houghton Mifflin Harcourt Publishing Company

$6 \times 9$

Hint:
What is $9 \times 6$?
© Houghton Mifflin Harcourt Publishing Company

$7 \times 2$

Hint:
What is $2 \times 7$?
© Houghton Mifflin Harcourt Publishing Company

$7 \cdot 3$

Hint:
What is $3 \cdot 7$?
© Houghton Mifflin Harcourt Publishing Company

$7 * 4$

Hint:
What is $4 * 7$?
© Houghton Mifflin Harcourt Publishing Company

$7 \times 5$

Hint:
What is $5 \times 7$?
© Houghton Mifflin Harcourt Publishing Company

$7 \times 6$

Hint:
What is $6 \times 7$?
© Houghton Mifflin Harcourt Publishing Company

$7 \cdot 7$

© Houghton Mifflin Harcourt Publishing Company

$7 * 8$

Hint:
What is $8 * 7$?
© Houghton Mifflin Harcourt Publishing Company

$7 \times 9$

Hint:
What is $9 \times 7$?
© Houghton Mifflin Harcourt Publishing Company

$6 \overline{)30}$

Hint: What is
$\square \times 6 = 30$?

© Houghton Mifflin Harcourt Publishing Company

$6 \overline{)24}$

Hint: What is
$\square \times 6 = 24$?

© Houghton Mifflin Harcourt Publishing Company

$6 \overline{)18}$

Hint: What is
$\square \times 6 = 18$?

© Houghton Mifflin Harcourt Publishing Company

$6 \overline{)12}$

Hint: What is
$\square \times 6 = 12$?

© Houghton Mifflin Harcourt Publishing Company

$6 \overline{)54}$

Hint: What is
$\square \times 6 = 54$?

© Houghton Mifflin Harcourt Publishing Company

$6 \overline{)48}$

Hint: What is
$\square \times 6 = 48$?

© Houghton Mifflin Harcourt Publishing Company

$6 \overline{)42}$

Hint: What is
$\square \times 6 = 42$?

© Houghton Mifflin Harcourt Publishing Company

$6 \overline{)36}$

Hint: What is
$\square \times 6 = 36$?

© Houghton Mifflin Harcourt Publishing Company

$7 \overline{)35}$

Hint: What is
$\square \times 7 = 35$?

© Houghton Mifflin Harcourt Publishing Company

$7 \overline{)28}$

Hint: What is
$\square \times 7 = 28$?

© Houghton Mifflin Harcourt Publishing Company

$7 \overline{)21}$

Hint: What is
$\square \times 7 = 21$?

© Houghton Mifflin Harcourt Publishing Company

$7 \overline{)14}$

Hint: What is
$\square \times 7 = 14$?

© Houghton Mifflin Harcourt Publishing Company

$7 \overline{)63}$

Hint: What is
$\square \times 7 = 63$?

© Houghton Mifflin Harcourt Publishing Company

$7 \overline{)56}$

Hint: What is
$\square \times 7 = 56$?

© Houghton Mifflin Harcourt Publishing Company

$7 \overline{)49}$

Hint: What is
$\square \times 7 = 49$?

© Houghton Mifflin Harcourt Publishing Company

$7 \overline{)42}$

Hint: What is
$\square \times 7 = 42$?

© Houghton Mifflin Harcourt Publishing Company

8 × 2

Hint:
What is 2 × 8?

8 • 3

Hint:
What is 3 • 8?

8 * 4

Hint:
What is 4 * 8?

8 × 5

Hint:
What is 5 × 8?

8 × 6

Hint:
What is 6 × 8?

8 • 7

Hint:
What is 7 • 8?

8 * 8

8 × 9

Hint:
What is 9 × 8?

×

•

*

×

×

•

*

×

You can write any numbers on the last 8 cards. Use them to practice difficult problems or if you lose a card.

Product Cards: 6s, 7s, 8s **149I**

Name Date

| | | | |
|---|---|---|---|
| $8\overline{)40}$<br>Hint: What is<br>$\square \times 8 = 40$?<br>© Houghton Mifflin Harcourt Publishing Company | $8\overline{)32}$<br>Hint: What is<br>$\square \times 8 = 32$?<br>© Houghton Mifflin Harcourt Publishing Company | $8\overline{)24}$<br>Hint: What is<br>$\square \times 8 = 24$?<br>© Houghton Mifflin Harcourt Publishing Company | $8\overline{)16}$<br>Hint: What is<br>$\square \times 8 = 16$?<br>© Houghton Mifflin Harcourt Publishing Company |
| $8\overline{)72}$<br>Hint: What is<br>$\square \times 8 = 72$?<br>© Houghton Mifflin Harcourt Publishing Company | $8\overline{)64}$<br>Hint: What is<br>$\square \times 8 = 64$?<br>© Houghton Mifflin Harcourt Publishing Company | $8\overline{)56}$<br>Hint: What is<br>$\square \times 8 = 56$?<br>© Houghton Mifflin Harcourt Publishing Company | $8\overline{)48}$<br>Hint: What is<br>$\square \times 8 = 48$?<br>© Houghton Mifflin Harcourt Publishing Company |
| $\overline{)\phantom{00}}$ | $\overline{)\phantom{00}}$ | $\overline{)\phantom{00}}$ | $\overline{)\phantom{00}}$ |
| $\overline{)\phantom{00}}$ | $\overline{)\phantom{00}}$ | $\overline{)\phantom{00}}$ | $\overline{)\phantom{00}}$ |



You can write any numbers on the last 8 cards. Use them to practice difficult problems or if you lose a card.

► PATH to FLUENCY **Diagnostic Checkup for Basic Multiplication**

1. $7 \times 5 =$ ___   2. $2 \times 3 =$ ___   3. $9 \times 9 =$ ___   4. $9 \times 6 =$ ___

5. $6 \times 2 =$ ___   6. $3 \times 0 =$ ___   7. $3 \times 4 =$ ___   8. $6 \times 8 =$ ___

9. $5 \times 9 =$ ___   10. $3 \times 3 =$ ___   11. $2 \times 9 =$ ___   12. $5 \times 7 =$ ___

13. $6 \times 10 =$ ___   14. $4 \times 1 =$ ___   15. $6 \times 4 =$ ___   16. $4 \times 8 =$ ___

17. $5 \times 2 =$ ___   18. $1 \times 3 =$ ___   19. $3 \times 9 =$ ___   20. $7 \times 6 =$ ___

21. $7 \times 2 =$ ___   22. $9 \times 0 =$ ___   23. $8 \times 9 =$ ___   24. $8 \times 7 =$ ___

25. $8 \times 10 =$ ___   26. $6 \times 3 =$ ___   27. $4 \times 4 =$ ___   28. $3 \times 8 =$ ___

29. $5 \times 5 =$ ___   30. $6 \times 0 =$ ___   31. $7 \times 9 =$ ___   32. $6 \times 6 =$ ___

33. $9 \times 2 =$ ___   34. $8 \times 3 =$ ___   35. $5 \times 4 =$ ___   36. $7 \times 7 =$ ___

37. $5 \times 10 =$ ___   38. $5 \times 1 =$ ___   39. $10 \times 9 =$ ___   40. $5 \times 6 =$ ___

41. $6 \times 5 =$ ___   42. $9 \times 3 =$ ___   43. $4 \times 2 =$ ___   44. $7 \times 8 =$ ___

45. $8 \times 2 =$ ___   46. $5 \times 0 =$ ___   47. $4 \times 9 =$ ___   48. $6 \times 7 =$ ___

49. $9 \times 5 =$ ___   50. $6 \times 1 =$ ___   51. $7 \times 4 =$ ___   52. $9 \times 8 =$ ___

53. $4 \times 10 =$ ___   54. $5 \times 3 =$ ___   55. $6 \times 9 =$ ___   56. $8 \times 6 =$ ___

57. $8 \times 5 =$ ___   58. $8 \times 0 =$ ___   59. $8 \times 4 =$ ___   60. $4 \times 7 =$ ___

61. $3 \times 5 =$ ___   62. $7 \times 3 =$ ___   63. $5 \times 9 =$ ___   64. $3 \times 6 =$ ___

65. $7 \times 10 =$ ___   66. $8 \times 1 =$ ___   67. $0 \times 4 =$ ___   68. $9 \times 7 =$ ___

69. $4 \times 5 =$ ___   70. $4 \times 3 =$ ___   71. $1 \times 9 =$ ___   72. $8 \times 8 =$ ___

► **PATH to FLUENCY** **Diagnostic Checkup for Basic Division**

1. 12 ÷ 2 = ___    2. 8 ÷ 1 = ___    3. 36 ÷ 9 = ___    4. 35 ÷ 7 = ___

5. 20 ÷ 5 = ___    6. 24 ÷ 3 = ___    7. 12 ÷ 4 = ___    8. 6 ÷ 6 = ___

9. 6 ÷ 2 = ___    10. 3 ÷ 3 = ___    11. 18 ÷ 9 = ___    12. 63 ÷ 7 = ___

13. 20 ÷ 10 = ___    14. 0 ÷ 1 = ___    15. 40 ÷ 4 = ___    16. 48 ÷ 8 = ___

17. 18 ÷ 2 = ___    18. 6 ÷ 3 = ___    19. 8 ÷ 4 = ___    20. 36 ÷ 6 = ___

21. 8 ÷ 2 = ___    22. 9 ÷ 1 = ___    23. 9 ÷ 9 = ___    24. 56 ÷ 7 = ___

25. 40 ÷ 5 = ___    26. 9 ÷ 3 = ___    27. 36 ÷ 4 = ___    28. 56 ÷ 8 = ___

29. 80 ÷ 10 = ___    30. 7 ÷ 1 = ___    31. 45 ÷ 9 = ___    32. 48 ÷ 6 = ___

33. 5 ÷ 5 = ___    34. 30 ÷ 3 = ___    35. 16 ÷ 4 = ___    36. 72 ÷ 8 = ___

37. 10 ÷ 2 = ___    38. 1 ÷ 1 = ___    39. 54 ÷ 9 = ___    40. 21 ÷ 7 = ___

41. 25 ÷ 5 = ___    42. 15 ÷ 3 = ___    43. 32 ÷ 4 = ___    44. 24 ÷ 8 = ___

45. 90 ÷ 10 = ___    46. 18 ÷ 3 = ___    47. 63 ÷ 9 = ___    48. 54 ÷ 6 = ___

49. 45 ÷ 5 = ___    50. 6 ÷ 1 = ___    51. 20 ÷ 4 = ___    52. 49 ÷ 7 = ___

53. 15 ÷ 5 = ___    54. 0 ÷ 3 = ___    55. 28 ÷ 4 = ___    56. 30 ÷ 6 = ___

57. 16 ÷ 2 = ___    58. 21 ÷ 3 = ___    59. 81 ÷ 9 = ___    60. 64 ÷ 8 = ___

61. 30 ÷ 5 = ___    62. 12 ÷ 3 = ___    63. 27 ÷ 9 = ___    64. 42 ÷ 7 = ___

65. 40 ÷ 10 = ___    66. 10 ÷ 1 = ___    67. 24 ÷ 4 = ___    68. 18 ÷ 6 = ___

69. 35 ÷ 5 = ___    70. 27 ÷ 3 = ___    71. 72 ÷ 9 = ___    72. 42 ÷ 6 = ___

▶ **PATH to FLUENCY** **Patterns With 10s, 5s, and 9s**

These multiplication tables help us see some patterns that make recalling basic multiplications easier.

1. What pattern do you see in the 10s count-bys?

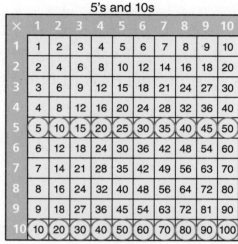

2. Look at the 5s and the 10s products together. What patterns do you see?

3. Look at the 9s count-bys. How does each 9s count-by relate to the 10s count-by in the next row?

   How could this pattern help you remember the 9s count-bys?

4. Look at the digits in each 9s product. What is the sum of the digits in each 9s product?

   How could you use this knowledge to check your answers when you multiply by 9?

▶ **PATH to FLUENCY** **Patterns With Other Numbers**

**On these grids, find patterns with 2s, 4s, 6s, and 8s.**

5. Look at the ones digits in all the 2s, 4s, 6s, and 8s count-bys. What pattern do you see?

6. Are the 2s, 4s, 6s, and 8s products even numbers or odd numbers?

2's, 4's, 6's, 8's

| × | 1 | 2 | 3 | 4 | 5 | 6 | 7 | 8 | 9 |
|---|---|---|---|---|---|---|---|---|---|
| 1 | 1 | 2 | 3 | 4 | 5 | 6 | 7 | 8 | 9 |
| 2 | 2 | 4 | 6 | 8 | 10 | 12 | 14 | 16 | 18 |
| 3 | 3 | 6 | 9 | 12 | 15 | 18 | 21 | 24 | 27 |
| 4 | 4 | 8 | 12 | 16 | 20 | 24 | 28 | 32 | 36 |
| 5 | 5 | 10 | 15 | 20 | 25 | 30 | 35 | 40 | 45 |
| 6 | 6 | 12 | 18 | 24 | 30 | 36 | 42 | 48 | 54 |
| 7 | 7 | 14 | 21 | 28 | 35 | 42 | 49 | 56 | 63 |
| 8 | 8 | 16 | 24 | 32 | 40 | 48 | 56 | 64 | 72 |
| 9 | 9 | 18 | 27 | 36 | 45 | 54 | 63 | 72 | 81 |
| 10 | 10 | 20 | 30 | 40 | 50 | 60 | 70 | 80 | 90 |

**On the multiplication table labeled Doubles, look for rows that have products that are double the product in other rows.**

7. Name the factors that have products that are double the products of another factor.

Doubles

| × | 1 | 2 | 3 | 4 | 5 | 6 | 7 | 8 | 9 |
|---|---|---|---|---|---|---|---|---|---|
| 1 | 1 | 2 | 3 | 4 | 5 | 6 | 7 | 8 | 9 |
| 2 | 2 | 4 | 6 | 8 | 10 | 12 | 14 | 16 | 18 |
| 3 | 3 | 6 | 9 | 12 | 15 | 18 | 21 | 24 | 27 |
| 4 | 4 | 8 | 12 | 16 | 20 | 24 | 28 | 32 | 36 |
| 5 | 5 | 10 | 15 | 20 | 25 | 30 | 35 | 40 | 45 |
| 6 | 6 | 12 | 18 | 24 | 30 | 36 | 42 | 48 | 54 |
| 7 | 7 | 14 | 21 | 28 | 35 | 42 | 49 | 56 | 63 |
| 8 | 8 | 16 | 24 | 32 | 40 | 48 | 56 | 64 | 72 |
| 9 | 9 | 18 | 27 | 36 | 45 | 54 | 63 | 72 | 81 |
| 10 | 10 | 20 | 30 | 40 | 50 | 60 | 70 | 80 | 90 |

8. How can you find $6 \times 8$ if you know $3 \times 8$?

**Rewrite each list of numbers so that it is a count by list.**

9. 4, 8, 12, 18, 20, 24, 28

10. 18, 28, 36, 45, 54, 63, 70

## ► Math and Recipes

The animal keepers at zoos feed and care for the animals. The animal keepers consult a zoo nutritionist to decide what and how much to feed the animals. In the zoo kitchens there are recipes posted for each type of animal such as the one shown below.

| **Gorilla Zoo Stew** | |
| --- | --- |
| 32 carrots | 8 yams |
| 32 oranges | 8 eggs |
| 24 apples | 16 bananas |
| 64 ounces Monkey Chow | 72 grapes |
| 48 ounces primate-diet food | 56 stalks of celery |
| 8 heads lettuce, any variety | bales of hydroponic grass to taste |

Toss all ingredients lightly. Divide among 8 trays.

The recipe makes 8 gorilla servings.

**Write an equation and solve the problem.**

1. How much of each ingredient is in 1 gorilla serving?

_____

_____

_____

2. How much of each ingredient in the Gorrilla Zoo Stew recipe is needed to serve 6 gorillas?

_____

_____

_____

► **Favorite Zoo Animals**

A third grade class took a field trip to a zoo.
The students were asked to name their favorite
zoo animal. The pictograph below shows the
animals the students chose.

**Favorite Zoo Animal**

| | |
|---|---|
| Bear | ☺ ☺ ☺ ☺ ☺ ☺ ☺ |
| Elephant | ☺ ☺ ☺ ☺ ☺ ☺ ☺ ☺ |
| Giraffe | ☺ ☺ ☺ ☺ |
| Gorilla | ☺ ☺ ☺ ☺ ☺ ☺ |
| Lion | ☺ ☺ |

Each ☺ stands for 7 students

3. Use the information in the pictograph to complete
the chart to show the number of students that chose
each zoo animal.

**Favorite Zoo Animal**

| Zoo Animal | Number of Students |
|---|---|
| Bear | |
| Elephant | |
| Giraffe | |
| Gorilla | |
| Lion | |

**Solve.**

4. If 63 students chose a zebra as their favorite zoo
animal, how many symbols would you use to show
that on the pictograph?

© Houghton Mifflin Harcourt Publishing Company

**VOCABULARY**
array
product
equal group
square number
multiple

## ► Vocabulary

**Choose the best word from the box.**

1. A(n) _____ is an arrangement of objects in columns and rows. **(Lesson 2-4)**

2. A(n) _____ is a product of a whole number and itself. **(Lesson 2-6)**

3. 80 is a(n) _____ of 10. **(Lesson 2-12)**

## ► Concepts and Skills

4. Explain how to use the order of operations to find the answer to this expression. Then find the answer. **(Lesson 2-10)**

$$3 + 4 \times 5 =$$

_____

_____

_____

5. Describe how to use mental math to find $90 \times 8$. **(Lesson 2-12)**

_____

_____

**Find the answer. (Lesson 2-10)**

6. $(7 - 4) \times 5 =$ _____        7. $4 + 18 \div 3 =$ _____

**Multiply or divide.**
**(Lessons 2-1, 2-3, 2-5, 2-6, 2-7, 2-8, 2-12, 2-14)**

8. $7 \times 8 =$ ☐        9. $6 \bullet 9 =$ ☐        10. $55 \div 1 =$ ☐

11. $72 \div 9 =$ ☐        12. $30 \times 0 =$ ☐        13. $49/7 =$ ☐

14. $4 \bullet 3 =$ ☐        15. $2 * 10 =$ ☐        16. ☐ $= 8 \times 8$

## Multiply or divide.

(Lessons 2-1, 2-3, 2-5, 2-6, 2-7, 2-8, 2-12, 2-14)

17. ☐ × 3 = 24    18. 28 ÷ ☐ = 4    19. 3 × 90 = ☐

20. ☐  6)‾24‾    21. ☐  7)‾42‾

## ► Problem Solving

**Write an equation and solve the problem.**

(Lessons 2-2, 2-4, 2-7, 2-9, 2-10, 2-11, 2-13, 2-15)

22. The area of Keshawn's garden is 64 square feet. Its width is 8 feet. What is the length of this garden?

_____

23. Carrie found 7 seashells at the beach. Her brother found 8 seashells. They divided the seashells equally among 3 people. How many seashells did each person get?

_____

24. Mr. Alberto has 48 students to divide into teams of 8. The number of teams will be divided equally for three high school students to coach at practice. How many teams will each high school student get?

_____

25. **Extended Response** Marci has 7 bean bag dolls. Lucy has 2 bean bag dolls. Janice has twice the number of dolls as Marci and Lucy combined. How many dolls does Janice have? Explain the steps you used to solve the problem. Then write an equation to show the steps.

_____

_____

Dear Family,

In this unit, students explore ways to measure things using the customary and metric systems of measurement.

The units of measure we will be working with include:

| U.S. Customary System | Metric System |
|---|---|
| **Length** | **Length** |
| 1 foot (ft) = 12 inches (in.) | 1 meter (m) = 10 decimeters (dm) |
| 1 yard (yd) = 3 feet (ft) | 1 meter (m) = 100 centimeters (cm) |
| 1 mile (mi) = 5,280 feet (ft) | 1 decimeter (dm) = 10 centimeters (cm) |
| **Capacity** | **Capacity** |
| 1 cup (c) = 8 fluid ounces (oz) | 1 liter (L) = 1,000 milliliters (mL) |
| 1 pint (pt) = 2 cups (c) | |
| 1 quart (qt) = 2 pints (pt) | |
| 1 gallon (gal) = 4 quarts (qt) | |
| **Weight** | **Mass** |
| 1 pound (lb) = 16 ounces (oz) | 1 kilogram (kg) = 1,000 grams (g) |

Students will solve problems that involve liquid volumes or masses given in the same unit by adding, subtracting, multiplying, or dividing and by using a drawing to represent the problem.

Students will also generate measurement data with halves and fourths of an inch such as hand spans and lengths of standing broad jumps and graph their data in a line plot.

You can help your child become familiar with these units of measure by working with measurements together. For example, you might estimate and measure the length of something in inches. You might use a measuring cup to explore how the cup can be used to fill pints, quarts, or gallons of liquid.

Thank you for helping your child learn important math skills. Please call if you have any questions or comments.

Sincerely,
Your child's teacher

© Houghton Mifflin Harcourt Publishing Company

This unit includes the Common Core Standards for Mathematical Content for Operations and Algebraic Thinking, CC.3.OA.3; Number and Operations in Base Ten, CC.3.NBT.2; Measurement and Data, CC.3.MD.1, CC.3.MD.2, CC.3.MD.3, CC.3.MD.4; and for all Mathematical Practices.

Estimada familia:

En esta unidad los niños estudian cómo medir cosas usando el sistema usual de medidas y el sistema métrico decimal.

Las unidades de medida con las que trabajaremos incluirán:

| Sistema usual | Sistema métrico decimal |
|---|---|
| **Longitud** | **Longitud** |
| 1 pie (ft) = 12 pulgadas (pulg)<br>1 yarda (yd) = 3 pies (ft)<br>1 milla (mi) = 5,280 pies (ft) | 1 metro (m) = 10 decímetros (dm)<br>1 metro (m) = 100 centímetros (cm)<br>1 decímetro (dm) = 10 centímetros (cm) |
| **Capacidad** | **Capacidad** |
| 1 taza (tz) = 8 onzas líquidas (oz)<br>1 pinta (pt) = 2 tazas (tz)<br>1 cuarto (ct) = 2 pintas (pt)<br>1 galón (gal) = 4 cuartos (ct) | 1 litro (L) = 1,000 mililitros (mL) |
| **Peso** | **Masa** |
| 1 libra (lb) = 16 onzas (oz) | 1 kilogramo (kg) = 1,000 gramos (g) |

Los estudiantes resolverán problemas relacionados con volúmenes de líquido o masas, que se dan en la misma unidad, sumando, restando o dividiendo, y usando un dibujo para representar el problema.

También generarán datos de medidas, usando medios y cuartos de pulgada, de cosas tales como el palmo de una mano y la longitud de saltos largos, y representarán los datos en un diagrama de puntos.

Puede ayudar a que su niño se familiarice con estas unidades de medida midiendo con él diversas cosas. Por ejemplo, podrían estimar y medir la longitud de algo en pulgadas. Podrían usar una taza de medidas para aprender cómo se pueden llenar pintas, cuartos o galones con líquido.

Gracias por ayudar a su niño a aprender destrezas matemáticas importantes. Si tiene alguna duda o algún comentario, por favor comuníquese conmigo.

Atentamente,
El maestro de su niño

© Houghton Mifflin Harcourt Publishing Company

**COMMON CORE**

Esta unidad incluye los Common Core Standards for Mathematical Content for Operations and Algebraic Thinking, CC.3.OA.3; Number and Operations in Base Ten, CC.3.NBT.2; Measurement and Data, CC.3.MD.1, CC.3.MD.2, CC.3.MD.3, CC.3.MD.4; and for all Mathematical Practices.

**VOCABULARY**
line segment

## ▶ Units of Length

**Circle length units and fractions of units to show the length of the line segment. Write the length.**

1.

_____

2.
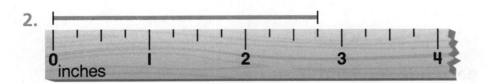

_____

3.
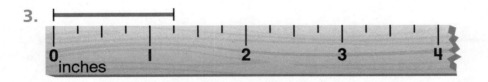

_____

4.
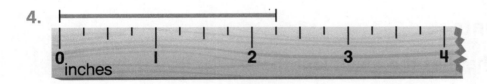

_____

5.

_____

6. **Why is this ruler wrong?**

_____

VOCABULARY
inch (in.)

## ▶ Estimate and Measure Length

**Estimate the length of each line segment in inches.**
**Then measure it to the nearest $\frac{1}{2}$ inch.**

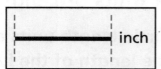

7. ‌

Estimate: _____    Actual: _____

8. ‌

Estimate: _____    Actual: _____

**Estimate the length of each line segment in inches.**
**Then measure it to the nearest $\frac{1}{4}$ inch.**

9. ‌

Estimate: _____    Actual: _____

## ▶ Draw Line Segments

**Draw a line segment that has the given length.**

10. 5 inches

11. $4\frac{1}{2}$ inches

12. $4\frac{3}{4}$ inches

13. Use a straightedge to draw a line segment that you
think will measure $2\frac{1}{2}$ inches long. Then use a ruler
to measure your line segment to the nearest $\frac{1}{4}$ inch.

**VOCABULARY**
**line plot**

## ▶ Line Plots with Fractions

A **line plot** shows the frequency of data on a number line. In science class, students measured the lengths of leaves in a leaf collection. They measured the lengths to the nearest $\frac{1}{4}$ inch. The line plot shows the results.

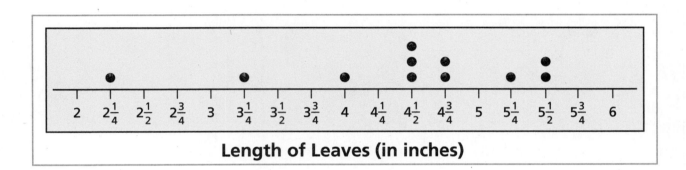

**Length of Leaves (in inches)**

**Use the line plot to answer the questions.**

14. How many leaves have a length of $4\frac{1}{2}$ inches? _____

15. How many leaves have a length that is less than 5 inches? _____

16. Write a question that can be answered using the line plot.

_____

_____

_____

## ► Make a Line Plot

**Your teacher will ask each student to read his or her actual measure for the line segments you and your classmates drew with a straightedge on Student Book page 160. Record the measures in the box below.**

17. Use the measurement data from the box above to complete the line plot below.

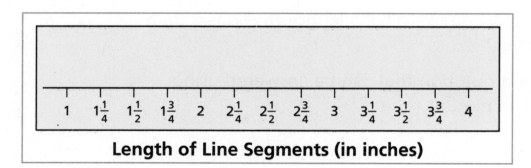

**Length of Line Segments (in inches)**

18. How many of the line segments have a measure of $2\frac{1}{2}$ inches?

_____

19. Which length appears the most often on the line plot?

_____

## ► Choose the Unit

**Choose the best unit to use to measure the
liquid volume. Write *cup*, *pint*, *quart*, or *gallon*.**

**1.** a carton of heavy cream

_____

**2.** a flower vase

_____

**3.** a swimming pool

_____

**4.** a wash tub

_____

## ► What's the Error?

Dear Math Students,

Today I had to choose the best unit
to use to measure how much water is
needed to fill a kitchen sink. I said the
best unit to use is cups. Is my answer
correct? If not, please correct my work
and tell me what I did wrong.

Your friend,
Puzzled Penguin

**5.** Write an answer to Puzzled Penguin.

_____

_____

_____

**6. Math Journal** Think of a container. Choose the unit
you would use to measure its capacity. Draw the
container and write the name of the unit you chose.
Explain why you chose that unit.

Name

Date

# ▶ Estimate Customary Units of Liquid Volume

**Ring the better estimate.**

7.

2 cups

2 quarts

8.

5 cups

5 gallons

9.

1 pint

1 gallon

10.

1 cup

1 pint

11.

1 cup

1 gallon

12.

30 cups

30 gallons

**Solve.**

13. Jamie makes a shopping list for a picnic with his four friends. He estimates that he'll need 5 quarts of lemonade for the group to drink. Do you think his estimate is reasonable? Explain.

_____

_____

_____

## ▶ Use Drawings to Solve Problems

**Use the drawing to represent and solve the problem.**

**14.** A painter mixed 5 pints of yellow and 3 pints of blue paint to make green paint. How many pints of green paint did he make?

_____

**15.** Ryan bought a bottle of orange juice that had 16 fluid ounces. He poured 6 fluid ounces in a cup. How many fluid ounces are left in the bottle?

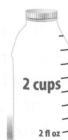

_____

**16.** A restaurant made 8 quarts of tea. They used all the tea to fill pitchers that hold 2 quarts each. How many pitchers were filled with tea?

_____

**17.** An ice cream machine makes 5 pints of ice cream in a batch. If 3 batches were made, how many pints of ice cream were made?

_____

**18.** Fran has a water jug that holds 24 quarts of water. She fills it with a container that holds 4 quarts. How many times must she fill the 4-quart container and pour it into the jug to fill the jug with 24 quarts?

_____

► **Solve Problems**

**Use the drawing to represent and solve the problem.**

*Show Your Work.*

19. Shanna bought 8 juice boxes filled with her favorite juice. Each box holds 10 fluid ounces. How many fluid ounces of her favorite juice did Shanna buy?

_____

20. Juana filled her punch bowl with 12 cups of punch. She gave some of her friends each a cup of punch. There are 7 cups of punch left in the bowl. How many cups did she give to friends?

_____

21. Mrs. Chavez made 20 quarts of pickles. She made 4 quarts each day. How many days did it take her to make the pickles?

_____

22. The sandwich shop began the day with 24 pints of apple cider. They sold 18 pints in the morning and the rest in the afternoon. How many pints of cider did they sell in the afternoon?

_____

23. A mid-sized aquarium holds 25 gallons of water and a large aquarium holds 35 gallons of water. How many gallons of water is needed to fill both aquariums?

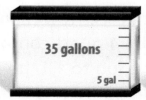

Name _____  Date _____

**VOCABULARY**
liquid volume
milliliter (mL)
liter (L)

► **Choose the Appropriate Unit**

**Choose the unit you would use to measure the
liquid volume of each. Write *mL* or *L*.**

1. a kitchen sink _____

2. a soup spoon _____

3. a teacup _____

4. a washing machine _____

**Circle the better estimate.**

5. a juice container    1 L        1 mL

6. a bowl of soup    500 L        500 mL

► **Use Drawings to Represent Problems**

**Use the drawing to represent and
solve the problem.**

7. There were 900 milliliters of water in a
pitcher. Terri poured 500 milliliters of
water into a bowl. How many milliliters
of water are left in the pitcher?

_____

8. Mr. Rojo put 6 liters of fuel into a gas
can that can hold 10 liters. Then he
added more liters to fill the can. How
many liters of fuel did he add to the can?

_____

9. Shelby needs to water each of her
3 plants with 200 milliliters of water. How
many milliliters of water does she need?

_____

## ► Make Sense of Problems Involving Liquid Volume

**Use the drawing to represent and solve the problem.**

10. The deli sold 24 liters of lemonade in 3 days. The same amount was sold each day. How many liters of lemonade did the deli sell each day?

_____

11. Tim has a bucket filled with 12 liters of water and a bucket filled with 20 liters of water. What is the total liquid volume of the buckets?

_____

12. Bella made a smoothie and gave her friend 250 milliliters. There are 550 milliliters left. How many milliliters of smoothie did Sara make?

_____

**Solve. Use a drawing if you need to.**

13. Diane has 36 cups of lemonade to divide equally among 4 tables. How many cups should she put at each table?

_____

14. Mr. Valle filled 7 jars with his famous barbeque sauce. Each jar holds 2 pints. How many pints of sauce did he have?

_____

## ► Choose the Appropriate Unit

**Choose the unit you would use to measure the weight of each. Write *pound or ounce*.**

**1.** a backpack full of books

_____

**2.** a couch

_____

**3.** a peanut

_____

**4.** a pencil

_____

**Circle the better estimate.**

| | | |
|---|---|---|
| **5.** a student desk | 3 lb | 30 lb |
| **6.** a television | 20 oz | 20 lb |
| **7.** a hamster | 5 oz | 5 lb |
| **8.** a slice of cheese | 1 lb | 1 oz |

## ► Use Drawings to Represent Problems

**Use the drawing to represent and solve the problem.**

**9.** Selma filled each of 3 bags with 5 ounces of her favorite nuts. How many ounces of nuts did she use altogether to fill the bags?

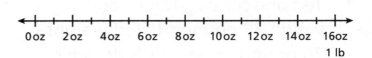

_____

**10.** Two apples together weigh 16 ounces. If one apple weighs 9 ounces, how much does the other apple weigh?

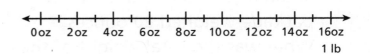

_____

## ► Use Drawings to Represent Problems (continued)

**Use the drawing to represent and solve the problem.**

11. Noah bought 16 ounces of turkey meat. If he uses 4 ounces to make a turkey patty, how many patties can he make?

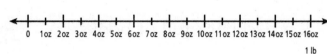

1 lb

_____

12. A package of silver beads weighs 6 ounces and a package of wooden beads weighs 7 ounces more. How much does the package of wooden beads weigh?

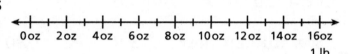

1 lb

_____

## ► Solve Word Problems

**Solve. Use a drawing if you need to.**

13. Ted and his dog together weigh 88 pounds. If Ted weighs 70 pounds, how much does his dog weigh?

_____

14. Emma has 20 ounces of popcorn kernels in a bag. If she pops 4 ounces of kernels at a time, how many times can Emma pop corn?

_____

15. Susan mailed 3 packages. Each package weighed 20 ounces. What was the total weight of the 3 packages?

_____

16. Bailey caught two fish. The smaller fish weighs 14 ounces and the larger fish weighs 6 ounces more. How much does the larger fish weigh?

_____

## ► Choose the Appropriate Unit

**Choose the unit you would use to measure the mass of each. Write *gram* or *kilogram*.**

**17.** an elephant

_____

**18.** a crayon

_____

**19.** a stamp

_____

**20.** a dog

_____

**Circle the better estimate.**

**21.** a pair of sunglasses    150 g         150 kg

**22.** a horse              6 kg          600 kg

**23.** a watermelon         40 g          4 kg

**24.** a quarter            500 g         5 g

## ► Use Drawings to Represent Problems

**Use the drawing to represent and solve the problem.**

**25.** Zach wants to buy 900 grams of pumpkin seed. The scale shows 400 grams. How many more grams does he need?

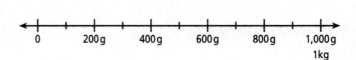

_____

**26.** Laura had 800 grams of fruit snacks. She put an equal amount into each of 4 containers. How many grams did she put in each container?

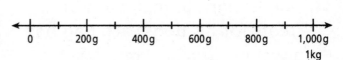

_____

## ▶ Solve Word Problems

**Use the drawing to represent and solve the problem.**

27. Nancy used 30 grams of strawberries and 45 grams of apples in her salad. How many grams of fruit altogether did she put in her salad?

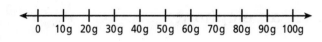

_____

28. Three people each donated a 20-kilogram bag of dog food to the animal shelter. How many kilograms of dog food was donated altogether?

_____

**Solve. Use a drawing if you need to.**

29. Barry weighs 40 kilograms and his younger brother weighs 25 kilograms. How much more does Barry weigh?

_____

30. Jolie made 3 necklaces that have a total weight of 180 grams. If each necklace weighs the same, how much would each necklace weigh?

_____

31. Dan bought 6 small bags of treats for his dog. Each bag has a weight of 40 grams. What is the total weight of all the bags?

_____

32. Carrie has a dog and a cat. Together they have a mass of 21 kilograms. If the cat has a mass of 9 kilograms, what is the mass of Carrie's dog?

_____

## ▶ What's the Error?

Dear Math Students,

Today I had to solve this problem: *Toby bought 3 bags of chips. Each bag of chips weighs 50 grams. What is the weight of all 3 bags of chips? Here is how I solved the problem.*

*50 + 3 = 53; 53 grams*

Is my answer correct? If not, please correct my work and tell me what I did wrong. How do you know my answer is wrong?

Your friend,
Puzzled Penguin

**33.** Write an answer to the Puzzled Penguin.

_____

_____

_____

_____

**Solve.**                                    *Show your work.*

**34.** A tennis ball weighs 60 grams. A golf ball weighs 45 grams. How many grams do the tennis ball and golf ball weigh altogether?

**35.** How many more grams does the tennis ball weigh than the golf ball?

**36.** Gary bought 10 slices of ham at the deli. Each slice weighed 2 ounces. How many ounces of ham did Gary buy?

**37.** Sadie had 40 grams of sunflower seeds. She divided the seeds evenly among her 5 friends. How many grams did each friend get?

## ► Choose the Better Estimate

**Circle the better estimate.**

**38.**

200 grams

200 kilograms

**39.**

10 kilograms

10 grams

**40.**

3 ounces

3 pounds

**41.**

100 pounds

10 ounces

**42.**

100 pounds

1 ton

**43.**

1 kilogram

10 kilograms

**Solve.**

44. Suzie estimated the weights of objects and ordered them by the estimates of their weights. She explained that estimating them was easy since the smallest objects weighed the least and the largest objects weighed the most. Do you agree with Suzie?

_____

Customary Units of Weight and Metric Units of Mass

► **Make Sense of Problems About Liquid Volume**

**Solve. Use drawings if you need to.**

*Show your work.*

1. Fran works in a science lab. She poured
   80 milliliters of liquid into each of 4 test tubes.
   How many milliliters of liquid did Fran pour into
   the test tubes altogether?

   _____

2. Nicholas wants to buy a bottle of shampoo.
   A large bottle has 375 milliliters of shampoo and
   a small bottle has 250 milliliters of shampoo.
   How many more milliliters of shampoo is in the
   larger bottle?

   _____

3. Allison used two containers of water to fill her
   aquarium. She used a container filled with 18 liters
   of water and another with 12 liters of water.
   What is the total liquid volume of the aquarium?

   _____

4. The coffee shop sold 28 liters of hot chocolate.
   If the same amount is sold each hour for 4 hours,
   how many liters of hot chocolate did the coffee
   shop sell each hour?

   _____

5. A recipe calls for 50 milliliters of milk. Eva has a
   spoon that holds 10 milliliters. How many times will
   Eva need to fill the spoon to follow the recipe?

   _____

## ▶ Make Sense of Problems About Masses

**Solve. Use drawings if you need to.**

*Show your work.*

6. A bag of green beans has a mass of 335 grams. A bag of peas has a mass of 424 grams. What is the total mass of both bags?

_____

7. An average sized chicken egg has a mass of 60 grams. What would be the total mass of a half dozen eggs?

_____

8. A kangaroo and her joey together have a mass of 75 kilograms. If the mother kangaroo has a mass of 69 kilograms, what is the mass of the joey?

_____

9. Liam and 2 of his friends have backpacks. The backpacks have masses of 6 kilograms, 4 kilograms, and 5 kilograms. What is the total mass of the three backpacks?

_____

10. Graham bought 4 bags of sunflower seeds. Each bag has 60 grams of seeds. Luke bought 3 bags of pumpkin seeds. Each bag has 80 grams of seeds. Who bought more grams of seeds, Graham or Luke? Explain.

_____

Dear Family,

In math class, your child is beginning lessons about time. This topic is directly connected to home and community and involves skills your child will use often in everyday situations.

Students are reading time to the hour, half-hour, quarter-hour, five minutes, and minute, as well as describing the time before the hour and after the hour.

For example, you can read 3:49 both as after and before the hour.

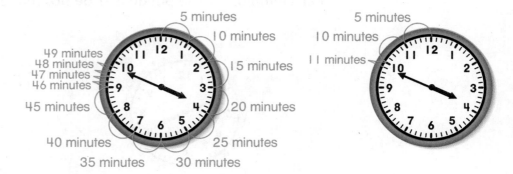

Forty-nine minutes after three

Eleven minutes before four

Students will be using clocks to solve problems about elapsed time.

Help your child read time and find elapsed time. Ask your child to estimate how long it takes to do activities such as eating a meal, traveling to the store, or doing homework. Have your child look at the clock when starting an activity and then again at the end of the activity. Ask how long the activity took.

Your child will also learn to add and subtract time on a number line.

If you have any questions or comments, please call or write to me.

Sincerely,
Your child's teacher

© Houghton Mifflin Harcourt Publishing Company

This unit includes the Common Core Standards for Mathematical Content for Operations and Algebraic Thinking, CC.3.OA.3; Number and Operations in Base Ten, CC.3.NBT.2; Measurement and Data, CC.3.MD.1, CC.3.MD.2, CC.3.MD.3, CC.3.MD.4; and for all Mathematical Practices.

Estimada familia:

En la clase de matemáticas su niño está comenzando lecciones que le enseñan sobre la hora. Este tema se relaciona directamente con la casa y la comunidad, y trata de destrezas que su niño usará a menudo en situaciones de la vida diaria.

Los estudiantes leerán la hora, la media hora, el cuarto de hora, los cinco minutos y el minuto; también describirán la hora antes y después de la hora en punto.

Por ejemplo, 3:49 se puede leer de dos maneras:

Las tres y cuarenta y nueve          Once para las cuatro

Los estudiantes usarán relojes para resolver problemas acerca del tiempo transcurrido en diferentes situaciones.

Ayude a su niño a leer la hora y hallar el tiempo transcurrido. Pídale que estime cuánto tiempo tomarán ciertas actividades, tales como comer una comida completa, ir a la tienda o hacer la tarea. Pida a su niño que vea el reloj cuando comience la actividad y cuando la termine. Pregúntele cuánto tiempo tomó la actividad.

Su niño también aprenderá a sumar y restar tiempo en una recta numérica.

Si tiene alguna pregunta o algún comentario, por favor comuníquese conmigo.

Atentamente,
El maestro de su niño

COMMON CORE

Esta unidad incluye los Common Core Standards for Mathematical Content for Operations and Algebraic Thinking, CC.3.OA.3; Number and Operations in Base Ten, CC.3.NBT.2; Measurement and Data, CC.3.MD.1, CC.3.MD.2, CC.3.MD.3, CC.3.MD.4; and for all Mathematical Practices.

**Name** _____    **Date** _____

### ▶ Make an Analog Clock

**Attach the clock hands to the clock face using a prong fastener.**

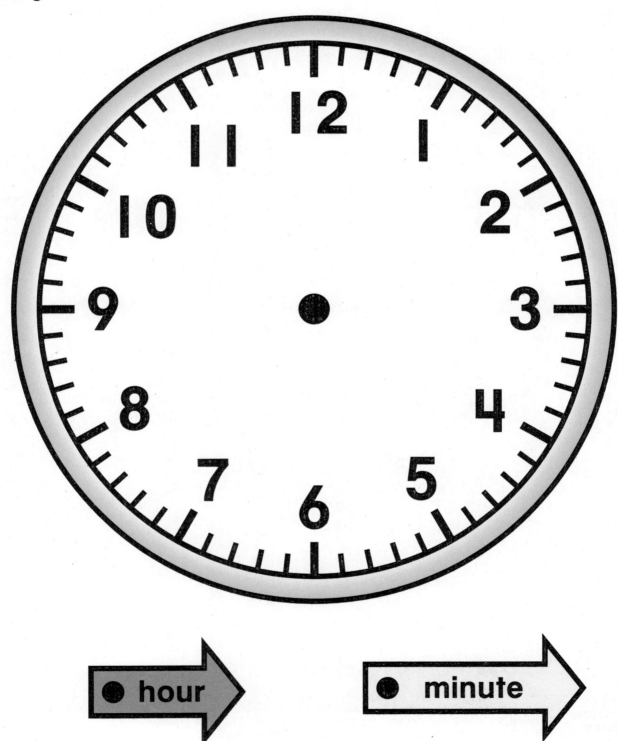

## ▶ Time to 15 Minutes

**Write the time on the digital clock. Then write how to say the time.**

1.

[ : ]

_____

2.

[ : ]

_____

3.

[ : ]

_____

4.

[ : ]

_____

**Write the time on the digital clock. Write two ways to say the time.**

5.

[ : ]

_____

_____

6.

[ : ]

_____

_____

7.

[ : ]

_____

_____

8.

[ : ]

_____

_____

9.

[ : ]

_____

_____

10.

[ : ]

_____

_____

11.

[ : ]

_____

_____

12.

[ : ]

_____

_____

## ▶ Show Time to 15 Minutes

**Draw the hands on the analog clock. Write the time on the digital clock.**

**13.** nine fifteen

[ _ : _ ]

**14.** half past seven

[ _ : _ ]

**15.** three o'clock

[ _ : _ ]

**16.** seven thirty

[ _ : _ ]

**17.** one forty-five

[ _ : _ ]

**18.** fifteen minutes after two

[ _ : _ ]

## ▶ Times of Daily Activities

**19.** Complete the table.

| Time | Light or Dark | Part of the Day | Activity |
|------|---------------|-----------------|----------|
| 3:15 A.M. | | | |
| 8:00 A.M. | | | |
| 2:30 P.M. | | | |
| 6:15 P.M. | | | |
| 8:45 P.M. | | | |

## ▶ Time to 5 Minutes

**Write the time on the digital clock. Then write how to say the time.**

20.

:

21.

:

22.

:

23.

:

24.

25.

26.

27.

**Write the time on the digital clock.**

28. ten minutes after eight

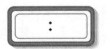
:

29. seven twenty-five

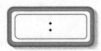
:

30. eleven fifty

:

31. six forty

32. five minutes after three

33. four fifty-five

## ▶ Time to 1 Minute

**Write the time on the digital clock. Then write how to say the time.**

34.

35.

36.

37.

38.

39.

40.

41.

**Write the time on the digital clock.**

42. ten fourteen

43. fifty-two minutes after eight

44. seven twenty-eight

45. nine thirty-one

46. forty-six minutes after eleven

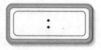

47. thirty-seven minutes after 5

**Name** _____  **Date** _____

## ► Times Before and After the Hour to 5 Minutes

**Write the time as minutes *after* an hour and minutes *before* an hour.**

**1.**

_____

_____

**2.**

_____

_____

**3.**

_____

_____

**4.**

_____

_____

**5.**

_____

_____

**6.**

_____

_____

**7.**

_____

_____

**8.**

_____

_____

**9.**

_____

_____

# ► Times Before and After the Hour to 1 Minute

**Write the time as minutes *after* an hour and minutes *before* an hour.**

10.

_____

_____

11.

_____

_____

12.

_____

_____

13.

_____

_____

14.

_____

_____

15.

_____

_____

16.

_____

_____

17.

_____

_____

18.

_____

_____

VOCABULARY
elapsed time

► **Elapsed Time in Minutes and Hours**

**1.** Find the **elapsed time**.

| Start Time | End Time | Elapsed Time |
|:---:|:---:|:---:|
| 4:00 P.M. | 7:00 P.M. | |
| 7:45 A.M. | 8:15 A.M. | |
| 2:17 P.M. | 7:17 P.M. | |
| 11:00 A.M. | 2:00 P.M. | |
| 11:55 A.M. | 4:25 P.M. | |

**2.** Find the end time.

| Start Time | Elapsed Time | End Time |
|:---:|:---:|:---:|
| 1:00 P.M. | 2 hours | |
| 4:15 A.M. | 4 hours | |
| 4:55 P.M. | 18 minutes | |
| 2:15 A.M. | 1 hour and 15 minutes | |
| 11:55 A.M. | 2 hours and 5 minutes | |

**3.** Find the start time.

| Start Time | Elapsed Time | End Time |
|:---:|:---:|:---:|
| | 3 hours | 4:15 P.M. |
| | 15 minutes | 2:45 P.M. |
| | 2 hours and 35 minutes | 11:55 A.M. |
| | 1 hour and 20 minutes | 3:42 A.M. |

► **Solve Problems About Elapsed Time on a Clock**

**Solve. Use your clock if you need to.**

*Show your work.*

4. Loretta left her friend's house at 3:45 P.M. She had been there for 2 hours and 20 minutes. What time did she get there?

_____

5. Berto spent from 3:45 P.M. to 4:15 P.M. doing math homework and from 4:30 P.M. to 5:10 P.M. doing social studies homework. How much time did he spend on his math and social studies homework?

_____

6. Ed arrived at a biking trail at 9:00 A.M. He biked for 1 hour and 45 minutes. He spent 20 minutes riding home. What time did he get home?

_____

7. Vasco cleaned his room on Saturday. He started at 4:05 P.M. and finished at 4:30 P.M. For how long did he clean his room?

_____

8. Mario finished swimming at 10:45 A.M. He swam for 1 hour and 15 minutes. What time did he start?

_____

9. Eric has basketball practice from 3:30 P.M. to 4:15 P.M. He has violin practice at 5:30 P.M. Today basketball practice ended 30 minutes late and it takes Eric 15 minutes to walk to violin practice. Will he be on time? Explain.

_____

## ► Add Time

**Solve using a number line.**                                    *Show your work.*

1. Keisha went into a park at 1:30 P.M. She hiked for 1 hour 35 minutes. Then she went to the picnic area for 45 minutes and left the park. What time did Keisha leave the park?

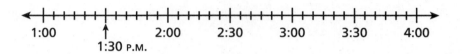

2. Loren arrived at the children's museum at 1:15 P.M. First, he spent 30 minutes looking at the dinosaur exhibit. Next, he watched a movie for 20 minutes. Then he spent 15 minutes in the museum gift shop. What time did Loren leave the museum? How long was he in the museum?

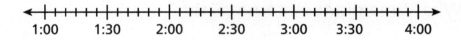

3. Caleb started working in the yard at 8:45 A.M. He raked for 1 hour 45 minutes and mowed for 45 minutes. Then he went inside. What time did he go inside? How long did he work in the yard?

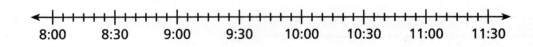

## ▶ Subtract Time

**Solve using a number line.**

4. Hank finished bowling at 7:15 P.M. He bowled for 2 hours 35 minutes. At what time did he start bowling?

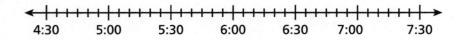

4:30    5:00    5:30    6:00    6:30    7:00    7:30

_____

5. Miguel has a job walking dogs. He finished walking the dogs at 7:10 P.M. He walked the dogs for 2 hours and 40 minutes. What time did Miguel start walking the dogs?

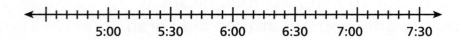

5:00    5:30    6:00    6:30    7:00    7:30

_____

6. The school music program ended at 8:35 P.M. It lasted for 1 hour 50 minutes. What time did the program start?

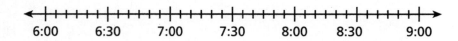

6:00    6:30    7:00    7:30    8:00    8:30    9:00

_____

7. Lia took bread out of the oven at 3:15 P.M. It baked for 35 minutes. She spent 15 minutes measuring the ingredients and 15 minutes mixing the batter. What time did Lia start making the bread?

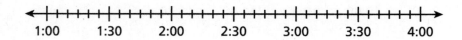

1:00    1:30    2:00    2:30    3:00    3:30    4:00

_____

Add and Subtract Time

► **Make Sense of Word Problems Involving Time Intervals**

**Solve. Use a clock or sketch a number
line diagram if you need to.**

*Show your work.*

1. Cory caught a train at 1:45 P.M. to go to his
   grandparents. The train trip lasted 35 minutes.
   Then he spent 10 minutes waiting for a cab
   and another 15 minutes riding in the cab. What
   time did Cory get to his grandparents' house?

   _____

2. Hirva left home at 9:45 A.M. and returned home
   at 11:20 A.M. She spent 55 minutes at the gym and
   the rest of the time at the library. How much time
   did Hirva spend at the library?

   _____

3. Diego arrived at soccer practice at 8:45 A.M.
   Practice lasted 45 minutes and then it took him
   10 minutes to walk home. What time did Diego
   get home?

   _____

4. Jan started working on her homework at 6:25 P.M.
   and she finished at 7:30 P.M. She spent 45 minutes
   on a book report and the rest of the time on math.
   How long did Jan spend on math?

   _____

5. Shanna finished her chores at 4:25 P.M. She spent
   35 minutes cleaning her room, 20 minutes bathing
   her dog, and 15 minutes folding clothes. What time
   did Shanna begin her chores?

   _____

▶ **What's the Error?**

Dear Math Students,

Today I was asked to find the time Jim got to
the doctor's office if he woke up at 7:55 A.M., spent
45 minutes getting dressed, and then drove
20 minutes to the doctor's office.

Here is how I solved the problem.

From 7:55 on a clock, I counted up 45 minutes to 8:45,
then I counted up 20 minutes to 9:05. Jim got to the
doctor's office at 9:05 A.M.

Is my answer correct? If not, please correct my work
and tell me what I did wrong. How do you know my
answer is wrong?

Your friend,
Puzzled Penguin

**6. Write an answer to the Puzzled Penguin.**

_____

_____

_____

**Solve.**

7. Wayne left home at 3:50 P.M. to go to the park. It took
30 minutes to drive to the park. He spent 45 minutes
at the park. What time did he leave the park?

_____

8. Leslie finished her project at 11:05 A.M. She spent 1 hour
10 minutes making a poster and 35 minutes writing a report.
What time did Leslie start her project?

_____

Dear Family,

In the rest of the lessons in this unit, your child will be learning to show information in various ways. Students will learn to read and create pictographs and bar graphs. They will organize and display data in frequency tables and line plots. Students will also learn how to use graphs to solve real world problems.

Examples of pictographs, bar graphs, and line plots are shown below.

**Birthday Cards Received**

| Bethany | ✉ ✉ ✉ ✉ |
| Raul | ✉ ✉ ✉ |
| Moishe | ✉ ✉ |
| Kirsten | ✉ ✉ ✉ ◁ |

Each ✉ stands for 4 cards.

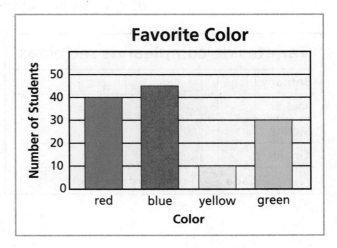

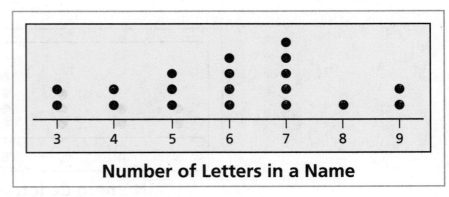

**Number of Letters in a Name**

Your child is learning how graphs are used in the world around us. You can help your child learn by sharing graphs that appear in newspapers, magazines, or online.

Thank you for helping your child learn how to read, interpret, and create graphs.

Sincerely,
Your child's teacher

**COMMON CORE**

This unit includes the Common Core Standards for Mathematical Content for Operations and Algebraic Thinking, CC.3.OA.3; Number and Operations in Base Ten, CC.3.NBT.2; Measurement and Data, CC.3.MD.1, CC.3.MD.2, CC.3.MD.3, CC.3.MD.4; and for all Mathematical Practices.

Estimada familia:

Durante el resto de las lecciones de esta unidad, su niño aprenderá a mostrar información de varias maneras. Los estudiantes aprenderán a leer y a crear pictografías y gráficas de barras. Organizarán y mostrarán datos en tablas de frecuencia y en diagramas de puntos. También aprenderán cómo usar las gráficas para resolver problemas cotidianos.

Debajo se muestran ejemplos de pictografías, gráficas de barras y diagramas de puntos.

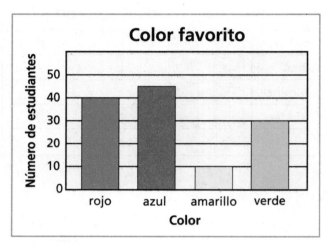

Su niño está aprendiendo cómo se usan las gráficas en la vida cotidiana. Puede ayudarlo mostrándole gráficas que aparezcan en periódicos, revistas o Internet.

Gracias por ayudar a su niño a aprender cómo leer, interpretar y crear gráficas.

Atentamente,
El maestro de su niño

© Houghton Mifflin Harcourt Publishing Company

COMMON CORE

Esta unidad incluye los Common Core Standards for Mathematical Content for Operations and Algebraic Thinking, CC.3.OA.3; Number and Operations in Base Ten, CC.3.NBT.2; Measurement and Data, CC.3.MD.1, CC.3.MD.2, CC.3.MD.3, CC.3.MD.4; and for all Mathematical Practices.

VOCABULARY
pictograph
key

## ► Read a Pictograph

A **pictograph** is a graph that uses pictures or symbols to represent data. The pictograph below shows the number of votes for favorite ice cream flavors. The **key** tells that each ice cream cone symbol stands for the way 4 students voted.

**Favorite Ice Cream Flavors**

| | |
|---|---|
| Peanut Butter Crunch | 🍦 🍦 |
| Cherry Vanilla | 🍦 🍦 🍦 |
| Chocolate | 🍦 🍦 🍦 🍦 🍦 |

Each 🍦 stands for 4 votes.

**Use the pictograph above to answer the questions.**

1. How many votes were there for chocolate?

2. How many people in all voted for their favorite ice cream flavor?

3. How many votes were there for Cherry Vanilla?

4. How many people did not vote for chocolate?

5. How many fewer votes were there for Peanut Butter Crunch than Chocolate?

6. How many more people voted for Chocolate than for Peanut Butter Crunch and Cherry Vanilla combined?

# ► Make a Pictograph

**7.** Use the data about Kanye's CDs to make your own pictograph.

| Kanye's CDs | |
|---|---|
| Type | Number of CDs |
| Jazz | 12 |
| Rap | 16 |
| Classical | 4 |

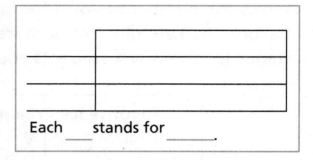

Each ____ stands for _____.

**8.** How many CDs in all does Kanye have?

_____

**9.** How many more rap CDs does Kanye have than classical?

_____

**10.** How many fewer jazz CDs does Kanye have than rap?

_____

**11.** How many pictures would you draw to show that Kanye has 9 Country and Western CDs?

_____

**VOCABULARY**
horizontal bar graph
vertical bar graph

### ► Read Bar Graphs

**Look at this horizontal bar graph and answer the questions.**

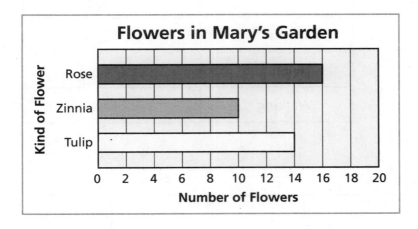

**Flowers in Mary's Garden**

Kind of Flower: Rose, Zinnia, Tulip
Number of Flowers: 0 2 4 6 8 10 12 14 16 18 20

**12.** What do the bars represent?

_____

_____

**13.** How many tulips are in Mary's garden?

_____

**Look at this vertical bar graph and answer the questions.**

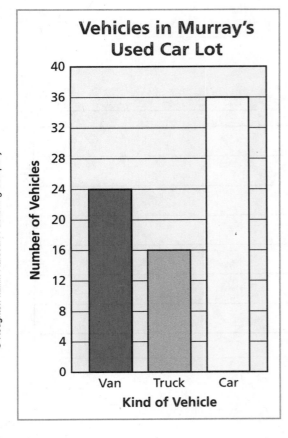

**Vehicles in Murray's Used Car Lot**

Number of Vehicles: 0 4 8 12 16 20 24 28 32 36 40
Kind of Vehicle: Van, Truck, Car

**14.** What do the bars represent?

_____

_____

_____

**15.** How many more vans than trucks are on Murray's Used Car Lot?

_____

## ▶ Create Bar Graphs

**16.** Use the information in this table to complete the horizontal bar graph.

| Favorite Way to Exercise | |
|---|---|
| Activity | Number of Students |
| Biking | 12 |
| Swimming | 14 |
| Walking | 10 |

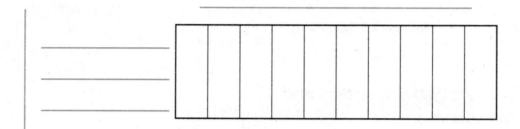

**17.** Use the information in this table to complete the vertical bar graph.

| Favorite Team Sport | |
|---|---|
| Sport | Number of Students |
| Baseball | 35 |
| Soccer | 60 |
| Basketball | 40 |

► Solve Comparison Problems Using Data in Pictographs

**Use the pictograph below to answer the questions.**

| What Musical Instrument Do You Play? | |
|---|---|
| Guitar | ♪ ♪ ♪ ♪ ♪ |
| Drums | ♪ ♪ ♪ ♪ ♪ ♪ ♪ ♪ ♪ ♪ |
| Piano | ♪ ♪ ♪ ♪ ♪ ♪ ♪ |
| Violin | ♪ ♪ ♪ |

Each ♪ = 4 students.

**18.** How many more students play guitar than violin?

_____

**19.** How many students do not play drums?

_____

**20.** Do more students play drums or guitar and violin combined?

_____

**21.** How many more students play guitar and piano combined than drums?

_____

**22.** Twelve fewer students play this instrument than drums.

_____

**23.** How many students in all were surveyed?

_____

# ► Solve Comparison Problems Using Data in Bar Graphs

**Use the bar graph below to answer the questions.**

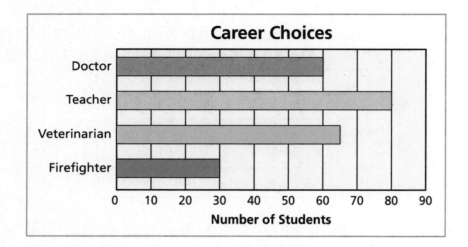

**24.** Twenty fewer students chose this career than teacher.

_____

**25.** Did more students choose veterinarian and firefighter combined or teacher?

_____

**26.** How many more students chose doctor than firefighter?

_____

**27.** How many students did not choose teacher?

_____

**28.** How many students in all were surveyed?

_____

**29.** How many more students chose doctor and firefighter combined than veterinarian?

_____

## ► Horizontal Bar Graphs with Multidigit Numbers

Use this horizontal bar graph to answer the questions below.

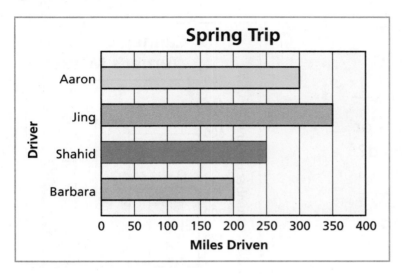

**Spring Trip**

1. How many miles did Shahid drive?

_____

2. Who drove 100 more miles than Barbara?

_____

3. How many more miles did Aaron and
Barbara combined drive than Jing?

_____

4. How many more miles did Shahid and
Aaron combined drive than Barbara?

_____

5. How many fewer miles did Barbara drive than Jing?

_____

6. Write another question that can be answered
by using the graph.

_____

_____

## ▶ Vertical Bar Graphs with Multidigit Numbers

**Use the vertical bar graph at the right to answer the questions below.**

7. How many cans of peas are at Turner's Market?

_____

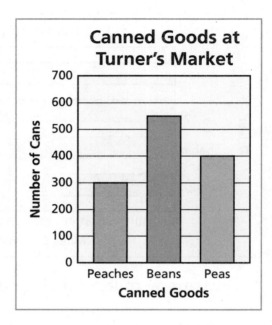

**Canned Goods at Turner's Market**

8. Are there more cans of beans or of peas and peaches combined?

_____

9. How many cans of beans and peaches are there altogether?

_____

10. How many more cans of beans are there than peas?

_____

11. How many fewer cans of peaches are there than peas and beans combined?

_____

12. Write another question that can be answered by using the graph.

_____

_____

_____

_____

## ► Create Bar Graphs with Multidigit Numbers

13. Use the information in this table to make a horizontal bar graph.

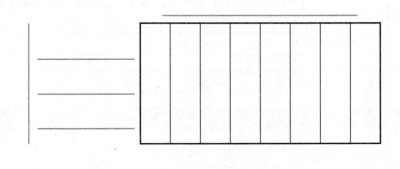

| Joe's DVD Collection | |
|---|---|
| **Type** | **DVDs** |
| Comedy | 60 |
| Action | 35 |
| Drama | 20 |

14. Use the information in this table to make a vertical bar graph.

| Summer Bike Sales | |
|---|---|
| **Type of Bike** | **Number Sold** |
| Road Bike | 200 |
| Mountain Bike | 600 |
| Hybrid Bike | 450 |

## ► Solve Problems Using Bar Graphs

Use the horizontal bar graph to answer
the questions below.

**Number of Visitors to Lost Creek Park**

15. There were how many more visitors to Lost Creek
Park in June than in May?

_____

16. How many visitors did the park have during the
months of May and June combined?

_____

17. The park had how many more visitors in July
than in August?

_____

18. Were there more visitors to the park in June
or in May and August combined?

_____

19. Write another question that can be answered
by using the graph.

_____

_____

## ▶ Frequency Tables and Line Plots

The ages of some players on a basketball team can be shown in different ways.

A **tally chart** can be used to record and organize data.

A **frequency table** shows how many times events occur.

A **line plot** shows the frequency of data on a number line.

| Tally Chart ||
|---|---|
| **Age** | **Tally** |
| 7 | I |
| 8 | III |
| 9 | ЖI |
| 10 | IIII |
| 11 | II |

| Frequency Table ||
|---|---|
| **Age** | **Tally** |
| 7 | 1 |
| 8 | 3 |
| 9 | 5 |
| 10 | 4 |
| 11 | 2 |

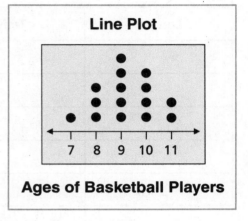

Line Plot

Ages of Basketball Players

## ▶ Make Sense of Data Displays

**Use the data displays above to answer Exercises 1–4.**

1. How many basketball players are 10 years old?

   _____

2. Which age appears the most often?

   _____

3. Are there more players younger than 9 or more players that are older than 9?

   _____

4. Write another question that can be answered by using the data displays.

   _____

   _____

# ► Create Line Plots with Fractions

1. Measure the length of the hand spans of 10 classmates to the nearest $\frac{1}{2}$ inch. Have your classmates spread their fingers apart as far as possible, and measure from the tip of the thumb to the tip of the little finger. Record the data in the tally chart below and then make a frequency table.

| Tally Chart | |
|---|---|
| **Length** | **Tally** |
| | |
| | |
| | |
| | |
| | |
| | |

| Frequency Table | |
|---|---|
| **Length** | **Tally** |
| | |
| | |
| | |
| | |
| | |
| | |

2. Use the data to make a line plot.

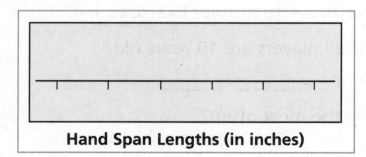

**Hand Span Lengths (in inches)**

3. Which length occurred the most often?

_____

4. Write a question that can be answered by using the data in the line plot.

_____

_____

## ► Solve Problems Using a Bar Graph

Five teams of students are riding their bikes after school
to raise money for the computer lab. Every completed
mile will earn the computer lab $2. The bar graph below
shows the number of miles completed in one week.

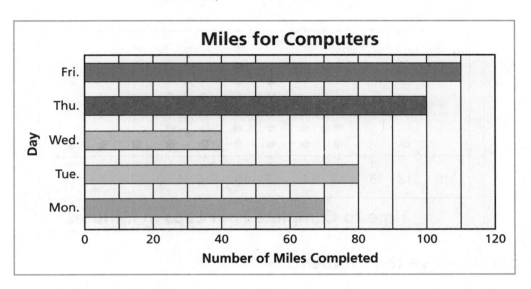

**Use the bar graph to solve the problems.**

1. How much money was earned
   for the computer lab on Tuesday?

   _____

2. How many fewer miles were
   completed on Monday than on
   Friday?

   _____

3. How many miles in all did the
   students ride?

   _____

4. How many more miles did students
   ride on Monday and Tuesday
   combined than on Friday?

   _____

5. There are four riders on each of
   the five teams. If each student
   completed the same number of
   miles, how many miles did each
   student ride on Wednesday?

   _____

6. Did students ride more miles
   on Monday and Wednesday
   combined or on Thursday?

   _____

© Houghton Mifflin Harcourt Publishing Company

## ▶ Solve Problems Using a Line Plot

The physical fitness coach asked her students to walk around a track four times. Four laps equal one mile. She recorded their times on the line plot below.

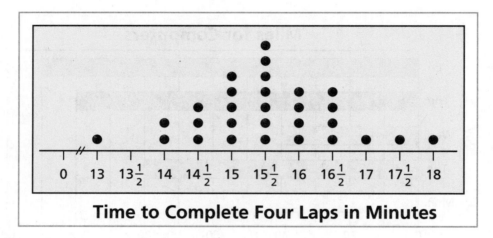

**Time to Complete Four Laps in Minutes**

**Use the plot to solve the problems.**

7. What is the difference between the greatest and the least amount of time students took to walk four laps?

_____

8. Did more students complete the laps in 16 minutes or more or in $15\frac{1}{2}$ minutes or fewer?

_____

9. How many students completed four laps in 16 minutes?

_____

10. The coach recorded the times of how many students?

_____

11. How many students completed four laps in fewer than 15 minutes?

_____

12. Most students completed the laps between which two times?

_____

Use Graphs to Solve Time and Measurement Problems

## ► Math and Sports

**Many students take part in a track and field day at school each year. One event is the standing broad jump. In the standing broad jump, the jumper stands directly behind a starting line and then jumps. The length of the jump is measured from the starting line to the mark of the first part of the jumper to touch the ground.**

**Complete.**

1. Your teacher will tell you when to do a standing broad jump. Another student should measure the length of your jump to the nearest $\frac{1}{2}$ foot and record it on a slip of paper.

2. Record the lengths of the students' jumps in the box below.

## ► How Far Can a Third Grader Jump?

**To analyze how far a third grader can jump, the data needs to be organized and displayed.**

3. Use the lengths of the students' jumps to complete the tally chart and the frequency table.

| Tally Chart | |
|---|---|
| Length | Tally |
| | |
| | |
| | |
| | |
| | |
| | |

| Frequency Table | |
|---|---|
| Length | Tally |
| | |
| | |
| | |
| | |
| | |
| | |

4. Make a line plot.

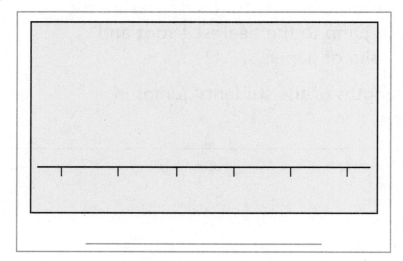

Focus on Mathematical Practices

VOCABULARY
elapsed time
liquid volume
mass
bar graph
line plot

## ▶ Vocabulary

**Choose the best word from the box.**

1. You can use a _____ to show data on a number line. **(Lesson 3-1)**

2. The amount of water in a bottle can be measured with a unit of _____. **(Lesson 3-2)**

3. The time that passes between the beginning and the end of an activity is _____. **(Lesson 3-8)**

## ▶ Concepts and Skills

4. If the hour hand is half-way between the 3 and 4 on a clock in the afternoon, what time is it? Explain. **(Lesson 3-6)**

   _____

   _____

5. When would you use kilograms to measure something. **(Lesson 3-4)**

   _____

   _____

6. Estimate the length of the marker in inches. Then measure it to the nearest $\frac{1}{4}$ inch. **(Lesson 3-1)**

   Estimate: _____    Actual: _____

**Write each time on the digital clock. Then write how to say the time.** (Lessons 3-6, 3-7)

7.

[ : ]

_____

8.

[ : ]

_____

**Circle the better estimate.** (Lessons 3-2, 3-3, 3-4)

9.

2 gallons
2 cups

10.

3 milliliters
3 liters

11.

2 kilograms
2 grams

**Use the table for Exercises 12 and 13.** (Lessons 3-11, 3-12)

| T-Shirt Sales | | | |
|---|---|---|---|
| Size | Small | Medium | Large |
| Number Sold | 40 | 70 | 50 |

12. Use the data in the table to complete the pictograph.

| T-Shirt Sales | |
|---|---|
| Small | |
| Medium | |
| Large | |
| Key: _____ | |

13. Use the data in the table to complete the bar graph.

## ► Problem Solving

**Use the bar graph below to solve problems 14 and 15.** (Lessons 3-11, 3-12)

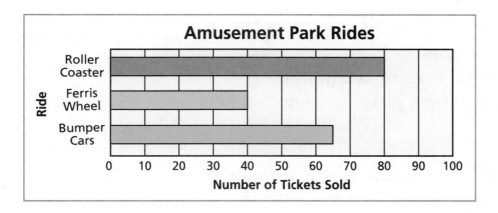

**Amusement Park Rides**

14. How many more tickets were sold for the roller coaster than bumper cars?

_____

15. How many tickets were sold altogether?

_____

**Solve.**

16. Kyle started his homework at 6:30 P.M. He spent 35 minutes on math and 40 minutes on a science report. What time did he finish his homework? How long did he spend doing homework? (Lessons 3-9, 3-10)

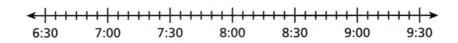

_____

17. At 6:45 Rico went to basketball practice. His practice lasted 1 hour and 20 minutes. What time did he finish practice? (Lesson 3-8)

_____

© Houghton Mifflin Harcourt Publishing Company

## ▶ Problem Solving

**Use the drawing to represent and solve the problem.**

18. Ariel picked some peaches.
    A peach has a mass of about
    150 grams. If the peaches
    she picked had a total mass of 600 grams,
    how many peaches did she pick? **(Lessons 3-4, 3-5)**

    0   100g 200g 300g 400g 500g 600g 700g 800g 900g 1000g
    1kg

    _____

19. Sue needs 100 milliliters of juice to make a batch
    of a juice drink. How many milliliters does she
    need to make 5 batches? **(Lessons 3-3, 3-5)**

    _____

    1 liter

    100 mL

20. **Extended Response**  A high school student
    measured the length of third graders' feet
    for a science project. The results are in the
    frequency table below. Use the frequency
    table to complete the line plot.
    **(Lessons 3-1, 3-3, 3-13, 3-14, 3-15)**

    What is the length of a typical third
    grader's foot in this survey? Explain
    why you chose that length.

    _____

    _____

line plot

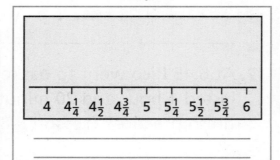

| **Frequency Table** | | | | | | | | |
|---|---|---|---|---|---|---|---|---|
| Length (in inches) | 4 | $4\frac{1}{4}$ | $4\frac{1}{2}$ | $4\frac{3}{4}$ | 5 | $5\frac{1}{4}$ | $5\frac{1}{2}$ | $5\frac{3}{4}$ | 6 |
| Number of Third Graders | 1 | 0 | 3 | 5 | 4 | 2 | 1 | 1 | 1 |

# Reference Tables

## Table of Measures

| Metric | Customary |
|---|---|

### Length/Area

| Metric | Customary |
|---|---|
| 1 meter (m) = 10 decimeters (dm) | 1 foot (ft) = 12 inches (in.) |
| 1 meter (m) = 100 centimeters (cm) | 1 yard = 3 feet (ft) |
| 1 decimeter (dm) = 10 centimeters (cm) | 1 mile (mi) = 5,280 feet (ft) |
| 1 square centimeter = 1 cm² | 1 square inch = 1 in² |
| A metric unit for measuring area. It is the area of a square that is one centimeter on each side. | A customary unit for measuring area. It is the area of a square that is one inch on each side. |

### Liquid Volume

| Metric | Customary |
|---|---|
| 1 liter (L) = 1,000 milliliters (mL) | 1 tablespoon (tbsp) = $\frac{1}{2}$ fluid ounce (fl oz) |
| | 1 cup (c) = 8 fluid ounces (fl oz) |
| | 1 pint (pt) = 2 cups (c) |
| | 1 quart (qt) = 2 pints (pt) |
| | 1 gallon (gal) = 4 quarts (qt) |

## Table of Units of Time

### Time

| | |
|---|---|
| 1 minute (min) = 60 seconds (sec) | 1 year = 365 days |
| 1 hour (hr) = 60 minutes | 1 leap year = 366 days |
| 1 day = 24 hours | |
| 1 week (wk) = 7 days | |
| 1 month, about 30 days | |
| 1 year (yr) = 12 months (mo) or about 52 weeks | |

## Properties of Operations

**Associative Property of Addition**

$$(a + b) + c = a + (b + c) \qquad (2 + 5) + 3 = 2 + (5 + 3)$$

**Commutative Property of Addition**

$$a + b = b + a \qquad 4 + 6 = 6 + 4$$

**Identity Property of Addition**

$$a + 0 = 0 + a = a \qquad 3 + 0 = 0 + 3 = 3$$

**Associative Property of Multiplication**

$$(a \cdot b) \cdot c = a \cdot (b \cdot c) \qquad (3 \cdot 5) \cdot 7 = 3 \cdot (5 \cdot 7)$$

**Commutative Property of Multiplication**

$$a \cdot b = b \cdot a \qquad 6 \cdot 3 = 3 \cdot 6$$

**Identity Property of Multiplication**

$$a \cdot 1 = 1 \cdot a = a \qquad 8 \cdot 1 = 1 \cdot 8 = 8$$

**Zero Property of Multiplication**

$$a \cdot 0 = 0 \cdot a = 0 \qquad 5 \cdot 0 = 0 \cdot 5 = 0$$

**Distributive Property of Multiplication over Addition**

$$a \cdot (b + c) = (a \cdot b) + (a \cdot c) \qquad 2 \cdot (4 + 3) = (2 \cdot 4) + (2 \cdot 3)$$

# Problem Types

## Addition and Subtraction Problem Types

| | Result Unknown | Change Unknown | Start Unknown |
|---|---|---|---|
| **Add to** | Aisha had 274 stamps in her collection. Then her grandfather gave her 65 stamps. How many stamps does she have now?<br><br>*Situation and solution equation:*[1]<br>$274 + 65 = s$ | Aisha had 274 stamps in her collection. Then her grandfather gave her some stamps. Now she has 339 stamps. How many stamps did her grandfather give her?<br><br>*Situation equation:*<br>$274 + s = 339$<br><br>*Solution equation:*<br>$s = 339 - 274$ | Aisha had some stamps in her collection. Then her grandfather gave her 65 stamps. Now she has 339 stamps. How many stamps did she have to start?<br><br>*Situation equation*<br>$s + 65 = 339$<br><br>*Solution equation:*<br>$s = 339 - 65$ |
| **Take from** | A store had 750 bottles of water at the start of the day. During the day, the store sold 490 bottles. How many bottles did they have at the end of the day?<br><br>*Situation and solution equation:*<br>$750 - 490 = b$ | A store had 750 bottles of water at the start of the day. The store had 260 bottles left at the end of the day. How many bottles did the store sell?<br><br>*Situation equation:*<br>$750 - b = 260$<br><br>*Solution equation:*<br>$b = 750 - 260$ | A store had a number of bottles of water at the start of the day. The store sold 490 bottles of water. At the end of the day 260 bottles were left. How many bottles did the store have to start with?<br><br>*Situation equation:*<br>$b - 490 = 260$<br><br>*Solution equation:*<br>$b = 260 + 490$ |

[1]A situation equation represents the structure (action) in the problem situation. A solution equation shows the operation used to find the answer.

| | Total Unknown | Addend Unknown | Both Addends Unknown |
|---|---|---|---|
| **Put Together/ Take Apart** | A clothing store has 375 shirts with short sleeves and 148 shirts with long sleeves. How many shirts does the store have in all?<br><br>*Math drawing:*<br><br>$s$<br>375   148<br><br>*Situation and solution equation:*<br><br>$375 + 148 = s$ | Of the 523 shirts in a clothing store, 375 have short sleeves. The rest have long sleeves. How many shirts have long sleeves?<br><br>*Math drawing:*<br><br>523<br>375   $l$<br><br>*Situation equation:*<br><br>$523 = 375 + l$<br><br>*Solution equation:*<br><br>$l = 523 - 375$ | A clothing store has 523 shirts. Some have short sleeves and some have long sleeves. How many of the shirts have short sleeves and how many have long sleeves?<br><br>*Math drawing:*<br><br>523<br>$s$   $l$<br><br>*Situation equation*<br><br>$523 = s + l$ |

*Problem Types continued*

## Addition and Subtraction Problem Types (continued)

| | Difference Unknown | Greater Unknown | Smaller Unknown |
|---|---|---|---|
| **Compare** | At a zoo, the female black bear weighs 175 pounds. The male black bear weighs 260 pounds. How much more does the male black bear weigh than the female black bear?<br><br>At a zoo, the female black bear weighs 175 pounds. The male black bear weighs 260 pounds. How much less does the female black bear weigh than the male black bear?<br><br>*Math drawing:* | **Leading Language**<br>At a zoo, the female black bear weighs 175 pounds. The male black bear weighs 85 pounds more than the female black bear. How much does the male black bear weigh?<br><br>**Misleading Language**<br>At a zoo, the female black bear weighs 175 pounds. The female black bear weighs 85 pounds less than the male black bear. How much does the male black bear weigh?<br><br>*Math drawing:* | **Leading Language**<br>At a zoo, the male black bear weighs 260 pounds. The female black bear weighs 85 pounds less than the male black bear. How much does the female black bear weigh?<br><br>**Misleading Language**<br>At a zoo, the male black bear weighs 260 pounds. The male black bear weighs 85 pounds more than the female black bear. How much does the female black bear weigh?<br><br>*Math drawing:* |

*Math drawing (Difference Unknown):*

```
| 260        |
| 175 | ( d )
```

*Situation equation:*

$175 + d = 260$ or

$d = 260 - 175$

*Solution equation:*

$d = 260 - 175$

*Math drawing (Greater Unknown):*

```
|     m      |
| 175 | (85)
```

*Situation and solution equation:*

$175 + 85 = m$

*Math drawing (Smaller Unknown):*

```
| 260        |
| f | (85)
```

*Situation equation*

$f + 85 = 260$ or

$f = 260 - 85$

*Solution equation:*

$f = 260 - 85$

A comparison sentence can always be said in two ways. One way uses *more*, and the other uses *fewer* or *less*. Misleading language suggests the wrong operation. For example, it says *the female black bear weighs 85 pounds less than the male*, but you have to add 85 pounds to the female's weight to get the male's weight.

# Multiplication and Division Problem Types

| | Unknown Product | Group Size Unknown | Number of Groups Unknown |
|---|---|---|---|
| **Equal Groups** | A teacher bought 5 boxes of markers. There are 8 markers in each box. How many markers did the teacher buy? | A teacher bought 5 boxes of markers. She bought 40 markers in all. How many markers are in each box? | A teacher bought boxes of 8 markers. She bought 40 markers in all. How many boxes of markers did she buy? |
| | *Math drawing:* | *Math drawing:* | *Math drawing:* |
| | *Situation and solution equation:* $n = 5 \cdot 8$ | *Situation equation:* $5 \cdot n = 40$  *Solution equation:* $n = 40 \div 5$ | *Situation equation* $n \cdot 8 = 40$  *Solution equation:* $n = 40 \div 8$ |

# Problem Types (continued)

| | Unknown Product | Unknown Factor | Unknown Factor |
|---|---|---|---|
| **Arrays** | For the yearbook photo, the drama club stood in 3 rows of 7 students. How many students were in the photo in all?<br><br>*Math drawing:*<br><br>7<br>3 ○○○○○○○<br>○○○○○○○<br>○○○○○○○<br><br>*Situation and solution equation:*<br><br>$n = 3 \cdot 7$ | For the yearbook photo, the 21 students in drama club, stood in 3 equal rows. How many students were in each row?<br><br>*Math drawing:*<br><br>( n )<br>( n )  Total: 21<br>( n )<br><br>*Situation equation:*<br><br>$3 \cdot n = 21$<br><br>*Solution equation:*<br><br>$n = 21 \div 3$ | For the yearbook photo, the 21 students in drama club, stood in rows of 7 students. How many rows were there?<br><br>*Math drawing:*<br><br>( 7 )<br>( 7 )  Total: 21<br>( 7 )<br><br>*Situation equation*<br><br>$n \cdot 7 = 21$<br><br>*Solution equation:*<br><br>$n = 21 \div 7$ |
| **Area** | The floor of the kitchen is 2 meters by 5 meters. What is the area of the floor?<br><br>*Math drawing:*<br><br>5<br>2 [ A ]<br><br>*Situation and solution equation:*<br><br>$A = 5 \cdot 2$ | The floor of the kitchen is 5 meters long. The area of the floor is 10 square meters. What is the width of the floor?<br><br>*Math drawing:*<br><br>5<br>w [ 10 ]<br><br>*Situation equation:*<br><br>$5 \cdot w = 10$<br><br>*Solution equation:*<br><br>$w = 10 \div 5$ | The floor of the kitchen is 2 meters wide. The area of the floor is 10 square meters. What is the length of the floor?<br><br>*Math drawing:*<br><br>$l$<br>2 [ 10 ]<br><br>*Situation equation*<br><br>$l \cdot 2 = 10$<br><br>*Solution equation:*<br><br>$l = 10 \div 2$ |

# Vocabulary Activities

## ▶ Word Review  `PAIRS`

Work with a partner. Choose a word from a current unit or a review word from a previous unit. Use the word to complete one of the activities listed on the right. Then ask your partner if they have any edits to your work or questions about what you described. Repeat, having your partner choose a word.

**Activities**

▶ Give the meaning in words or gestures.

▶ Use the word in the sentence.

▶ Give another word that is related to the word in some way and explain the relationship.

## ▶ Crossword Puzzle  `PAIRS` OR `INDIVIDUALS`

Create a crossword puzzle similar to the example below. Use vocabulary words from the unit. You can add other related words, too. Challenge your partner to solve the puzzle.

**Across**

1. _____ and subtraction are inverse operations.

2. To put amounts together

3. When you trade 10 ones for 1 ten, you _____.

4. The answer to an addition problem

**Down**

1. In 24 + 65 = 89, 24 is an _____.

3. A combination of the digits 0, 1, 2, 3, 4, 5, 6, 7, 8, and 9.

4. The operation that you can use to find out how much more one number is than another.

# Vocabulary Activities (continued)

## ▶ Word Wall  `PAIRS` OR `SMALL GROUPS`

With your teacher's permission, start a word wall in your classroom. As you work through each lesson, put the math vocabulary words on index cards and place them on the word wall. You can work with a partner or a small group choosing a word and giving the definition.

## ▶ Word Web  `INDIVIDUALS`

Make a word web for a word or words you do not understand in a unit. Fill in the web with words or phrases that are related to the vocabulary word.

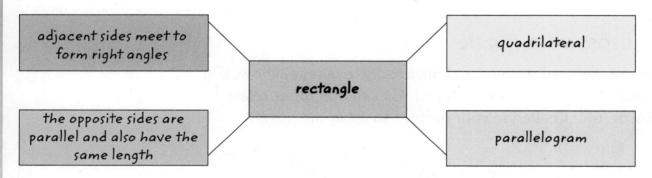

adjacent sides meet to form right angles

the opposite sides are parallel and also have the same length

rectangle

quadrilateral

parallelogram

## ▶ Alphabet Challenge  `PAIRS` OR `INDIVIDUALS`

Take an alphabet challenge. Choose 3 letters from the alphabet. Think of three vocabulary words for each letter. Then write the definition or draw an example for each word.

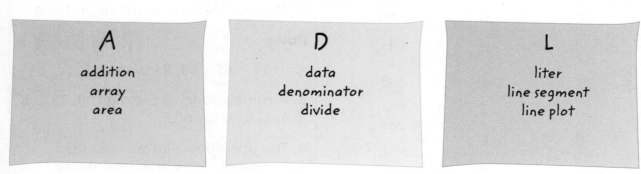

**A**
addition
array
area

**D**
data
denominator
divide

**L**
liter
line segment
line plot

## ► Concentration   PAIRS

Write the vocabulary words and related words from a unit on index cards. Write the definitions on a different set of index cards. Mix up both sets of cards. Then place the cards facedown on a table in an array, for example, 3 by 3 or 3 by 4. Take turns turning over two cards. If one card is a word and one card is a definition that matches the word, take the pair. Continue until each word has been matched with its definition.

|  |  |  |
|---|---|---|
| *area* |  |  |
|  |  | the number of square units in a region |
|  |  |  |

## ► Math Journal   INDIVIDUALS

As you learn new words, write them in your Math Journal. Write the definition of the word and include a sketch or an example. As you learn new information about the word, add notes to your definition.

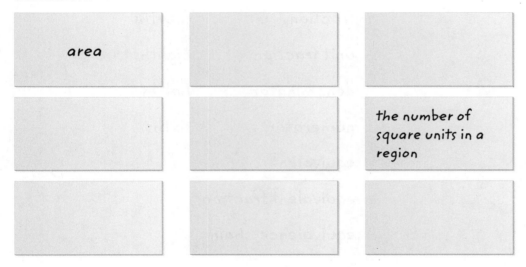

polygon: a closed plane figure with sides made of straight line segments.

In concave polygons, there exists a line segment with endpoints inside the polygon and a point on the line segment that is outside the polygon.

## ▶ What's the Word?  `PAIRS`

Work together to make a poster or bulletin board display of
the words in a unit. Write definitions on a set of index cards.
Mix up the cards. Work with a partner, choosing a definition
from the index cards. Have your partner point to the word
on the poster and name the matching math vocabulary word.
Switch roles and try the activity again.

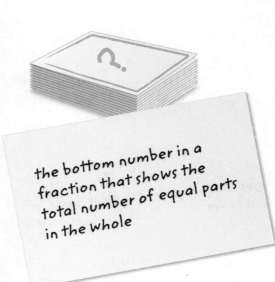

fraction          fourths

unit fraction     eighths

denominator       halves

numerator         sixths

equivalent

equivalent fractions

equivalence chain

thirds

the bottom number in a
fraction that shows the
total number of equal parts
in the whole

# Glossary

**addend** One of two or more numbers to be added together to find a sum.

Example: $8 + 4 = 12$

addend   addend   sum

**addition** A mathematical operation that combines two or more numbers.

Example: $23 + 52 = 75$

addend   addend   sum

**adjacent (sides)** Two sides of a figure that meet at a point.

Example: Sides $a$ and $b$ are adjacent.

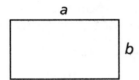

**A.M.** The time period between midnight and noon.

**analog clock** A clock with a face and hands.

**angle** A figure formed by two rays or two line segments that meet at an endpoint.

**area** The total number of square units that cover a figure.

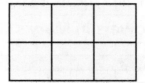

Example: The area of the rectangle is 6 square units.

**array** An arrangement of objects, pictures, or numbers in columns and rows.

**Associative Property of Addition (Grouping Property of Addition)**

The property which states that changing the way in which addends are grouped does not change the sum.

Example: $(2 + 3) + 1 = 2 + (3 + 1)$

$$5 + 1 = 2 + 4$$
$$6 = 6$$

**Associative Property of Multiplication (Grouping Property of Multiplication)**

The property which states that changing the way in which factors are grouped does not change the product.

Example: $(2 \times 3) \times 4 = 2 \times (3 \times 4)$

$$6 \times 4 = 2 \times 12$$
$$24 = 24$$

# Glossary (continued)

**axis (plural: axes)** A reference line for a graph. A graph has 2 axes; one is horizontal and the other is vertical.

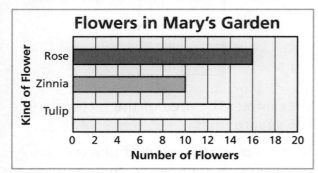

**Flowers in Mary's Garden**

---

**B**

**bar graph** A graph that uses bars to show data. The bars may be horizontal, as in the graph above, or vertical, as in the graph below.

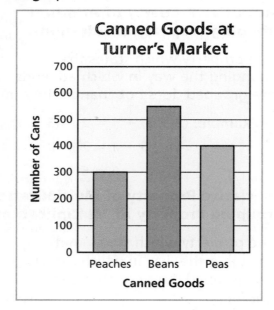

---

**C**

**capacity** The amount a container can hold.

**centimeter (cm)** A metric unit used to measure length.

100 centimeters = 1 meter

**column** A part of a table or array that contains items arranged vertically.

● ● ● ●
● ● ● ●
● ● ● ●
● ● ● ●

**Commutative Property of Addition (Order Property of Addition)** The property which states that changing the order of addends does not change the sum.

Example: $3 + 7 = 7 + 3$

$10 = 10$

**Commutative Property of Multiplication (Order Property of Multiplication)** The property which states that changing the order of factors does not change the product.

Example: $5 \times 4 = 4 \times 5$

$20 = 20$

**comparison bars** Bars that represent the greater amount, lesser amount, and difference in a comparison problem.

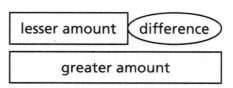

**concave** A polygon for which you can connect two points inside the polygon with a segment that passes outside the polygon.

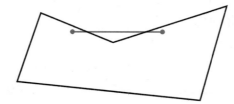

**convex** A polygon is convex if all of its diagonals are inside it.

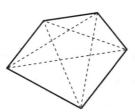

**cup (c)** A customary unit of measure used to measure capacity.

1 cup = 8 fluid ounces
2 cups = 1 pint
4 cups = 1 quart
16 cups = 1 gallon

## D

**data** Pieces of information.

**decagon** A polygon with 10 sides.

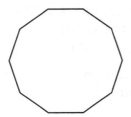

**decimeter (dm)** A metric unit used to measure length

1 decimeter = 10 centimeters

**denominator** The bottom number in a fraction that shows the total number of equal parts in the whole.

Example: $\frac{1}{3}$ ← denominator

**diagonal** A line segment that connects two corners of a figure and is not a side of the figure.

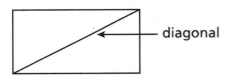
diagonal

**difference** The result of subtraction or of comparing.

**digit** Any of the symbols 0, 1, 2, 3, 4, 5, 6, 7, 8, 9.

**digital clock** A clock that displays the hour and minutes with numbers.

**Distributive property** You can multiply a sum by a number, or multiply each addend by the number and add the products; the result is the same.

Example:

$$3 \times (2 + 4) = (3 \times 2) + (3 \times 4)$$
$$3 \times 6 = 6 + 12$$
$$18 = 18$$

**dividend** The number that is divided in division.

Examples:

$$12 \div 3 = 4 \qquad 3\overline{)12}^{\,4}$$

dividend          dividend

**division** The mathematical operation that separates an amount into smaller equal groups to find the number of groups or the number in each group.

Example: $12 \div 3 = 4$ is a division number sentence.

**divisor** The number that you divide by in division.

Example: $12 \div 3 = 4 \qquad 3\overline{)12}^{\,4}$

divisor    divisor

# Glossary (continued)

## E

**elapsed time** The time that passes between the beginning and the end of an activity.

**endpoint** The point at either end of a line segment or the beginning point of a ray.

endpoint   endpoint   endpoint

**equation** A mathematical sentence with an equals sign.

Examples: $11 + 22 = 33$
$\qquad\qquad 75 - 25 = 50$

**equivalent** Equal, or naming the same amount.

**equivalent fractions** Fractions that name the same amount.

Example: $\frac{1}{2}$ and $\frac{2}{4}$

equivalent fractions

**estimate** About how many or about how much.

**even number** A whole number that is a multiple of 2. The ones digit in an even number is 0, 2, 4, 6, or 8.

## expanded form

**expanded form** A number written to show the value of each of its digits.

Examples:
$347 = 300 + 40 + 7$
$347 = 3 \text{ hundreds} + 4 \text{ tens} + 7 \text{ ones}$

**expression** A combination of numbers, variables, and/or operation signs. An expression does not have an equals sign.

Examples: $4 + 7 \qquad a - 3$

## F

**factors** Numbers that are multiplied to give a product.

Example:  $4 \times 5 = 20$

factor   factor   product

**fluid ounce (fl oz)** A unit of liquid volume in the customary system that equals $\frac{1}{8}$ cup or 2 tablespoons.

**foot (ft)** A customary unit used to measure length.

1 foot = 12 inches

**fraction** A number that names part of a whole or part of a set.

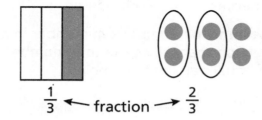

$\frac{1}{3}$ ← fraction → $\frac{2}{3}$

**frequency table** A table that shows how many times each event, item, or category occurs.

| Frequency Table | |
|---|---|
| **Age** | **Tally** |
| 7 | 1 |
| 8 | 3 |
| 9 | 5 |
| 10 | 4 |
| 11 | 2 |

**function table** A table of ordered pairs that shows a function.

For every input number, there is only one possible output number.

| Rule: add 2 | |
|---|---|
| **Input** | **Output** |
| 1 | 3 |
| 2 | 4 |
| 3 | 5 |
| 4 | 6 |

G

**gallon (gal)** A customary unit used to measure capacity.

1 gallon = 4 quarts = 8 pints = 16 cups

**gram (g)** A metric unit of mass. One paper clip has a mass of about 1 gram.

1,000 grams = 1 kilogram

**greater than (>)** A symbol used to compare two numbers.

Example: 6 > 5
        6 *is greater than* 5.

**group** To combine numbers to form new tens, hundreds, thousands, and so on.

H

**height** A vertical distance, or how tall something is.

**hexagon** A polygon with six sides.

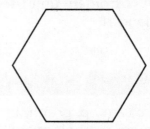

**horizontal** Extending in two directions, left and right.

**horizontal bar graph** A bar graph with horizontal bars.

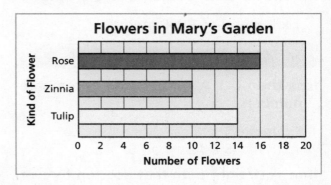

I

**Identity Property of Addition** If 0 is added to a number, the sum equals that number.

Example: 3 + 0 = 3

**Identity Property of Multiplication** The product of 1 and any number equals that number.

Example: 10 × 1 = 10

© Houghton Mifflin Harcourt Publishing Company

# Glossary (continued)

**improper fraction** A fraction in which the numerator is equal to or is greater than the denominator. Improper fractions are equal to or greater than 1. $\frac{5}{5}$ and $\frac{8}{3}$ are improper fractions.

**inch (in.)** A customary unit used to measure length.

12 inches = 1 foot

## K

**key** A part of a map, graph, or chart that explains what symbols mean.

**kilogram (kg)** A metric unit of mass.

1 kilogram = 1,000 grams

**kilometer (km)** A metric unit of length.

1 kilometer = 1,000 meters

## L

**less than (<)** A symbol used to compare numbers.

Example: 5 < 6
         5 *is less than* 6.

**line** A straight path that goes on forever in opposite directions.

**line plot** A diagram that shows frequency of data on a number line. Also called a *dot plot*.

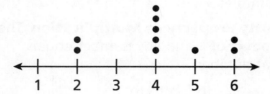

**line segment** A part of a line. A line segment has two endpoints.

**liquid volume** A measure of how much a container can hold. Also called *capacity*.

**liter (L)** A metric unit used to measure capacity.

1 liter = 1,000 milliliters

## M

**mass** The amount of matter in an object.

**mental math** A way to solve problems without using pencil and paper or a calculator.

**meter (m)** A metric unit used to measure length.

1 meter = 100 centimeters

**method** A procedure, or way, of doing something.

**mile (mi)** A customary unit of length.

1 mile = 5,280 feet

**milliliter (mL)** A metric unit used to measure capacity.

1,000 milliliters = 1 liter

**mixed number** A whole number and a fraction.

$1\frac{3}{4}$ is a mixed number.

**multiple** A number that is the product of the given number and any whole number.

**multiplication** A mathematical operation that combines equal groups.

Example: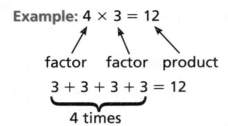

**N**

**number line** A line on which numbers are assigned to lengths.

**numerator** The top number in a fraction that shows the number of equal parts counted.

Example: $\frac{1}{3}$ ← numerator

**O**

**octagon** A polygon with eight sides.

**odd number** A whole number that is not a multiple of 2. The ones digit in an odd number is 1, 3, 5, 7, or 9.

**opposite sides** Sides of a polygon that are across from each other; they do not meet at a point.

Example: Sides *a* and *c* are opposite.

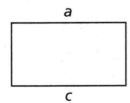

**Order of operations** A set of rules that state the order in which the operations in an expression should be done.

**STEP 1:** Perform operations inside parentheses first.

**STEP 2:** Multiply and divide from left to right.

**STEP 3:** Add and subtract from left to right.

**ounce (oz)** A customary unit used to measure weight.

16 ounces = 1 pound

**P**

**parallel lines** Two lines that are the same distance apart.

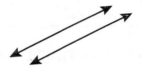

**parallelogram** A quadrilateral with both pairs of opposite sides parallel.

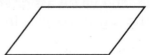

**pentagon** A polygon with five sides.

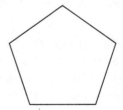

# Glossary (continued)

**perimeter** The distance around a figure.

Example:

Perimeter = 3 cm + 5 cm + 3 cm + 5 cm = 16 cm

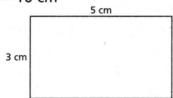

**pictograph** A graph that uses pictures or symbols to represent data.

**pint (pt)** A customary unit used to measure capacity.

1 pint = 2 cups

**place value** The value assigned to the place that a digit occupies in a number.

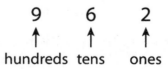

**place value drawing** A drawing that represents a number. Hundreds are represented by boxes, tens by vertical lines, and ones by small circles.

**P.M.** The time period between noon and midnight.

**polygon** A closed plane figure with sides made up of straight line segments.

**pound (lb)** A customary unit used to measure weight.

1 pound = 16 ounces

**product** The answer when you multiply numbers.

Example: 4 × 7 = 28

factor    factor    product

**proof drawing** A drawing used to show that an answer is correct.

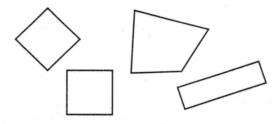

## Q

**quadrilateral** A polygon with four sides.

**quart (qt)** A customary unit used to measure capacity.

1 quart = 4 cups

**quotient** The answer when you divide numbers.

Examples:

35 ÷ 7 = 5

quotient

$7\overline{)35}$ ← quotient

**ray** A part of a line that has one endpoint and goes on forever in one direction.

**rectangle** A parallelogram that has 4 right angles.

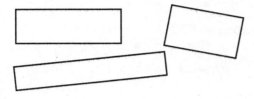

**rhombus** A parallelogram with equal sides.

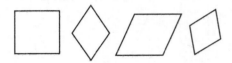

**right angle** An angle that measures 90°.

**round** To find about how many or how much by expressing a number to the nearest ten, hundred, thousand, and so on.

**row** A part of a table or array that contains items arranged horizontally.

**scale** An arrangement of numbers in order with equal intervals.

**side (of a figure)** One of the line segments that make up a polygon.

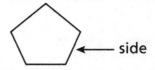
side

**simplify** To write an equivalent fraction with a smaller numerator and denominator.

**situation equation** An equation that shows the action or the relationship in a problem.

Example: $35 + n = 40$

**solution equation** An equation that shows the operation to perform in order to solve the problem.

Example: $n = 40 - 35$

**square** A rectangle with four sides of the same length.

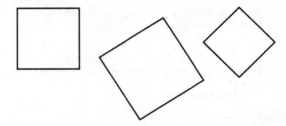

**square number** The product of a whole number and itself.

Example: $4 \times 4 = 16$

square number

# Glossary (continued)

**square unit** A unit of area equal to the area of a square with one-unit sides.

**standard form** The name of a number written using digits.

Example: 1,829

**subtract** To find the difference of two numbers.

Example: 18 − 11 = 7

**subtraction** A mathematical operation on two numbers that gives the difference.

Example: 43 − 40 = 3

**sum** The answer when adding two or more addends.

Example: 37 + 52 = 89

addend   addend   sum

## T

**table** An easy-to-read arrangement of data, usually in rows and columns.

| Favorite Team Sport | |
| --- | --- |
| Sport | Number of Students |
| Baseball | 35 |
| Soccer | 60 |
| Basketball | 40 |

**tally marks** Short line segments drawn in groups of 5. Each mark, including the slanted mark, stands for 1 unit.

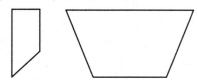 means 13
5   5   3

**total** The answer when adding two or more addends. The sum of two or more numbers.

Example: 672 + 228 = 900

addend   addend   total sum

**trapezoid** A quadrilateral with exactly one pair of parallel sides.

**triangle** A polygon with three sides.

## U

**ungroup** To open up 1 in a given place to make 10 of the next smaller place value in order to subtract.

**unit fraction** A fraction whose numerator is 1. It shows one equal part of a whole.

Example: $\frac{1}{4}$

**unit square** A square whose area is 1 square unit.

## V

**variable** A letter or symbol used to represent an unknown number in an algebraic expression or equation.

**Example:** $2 + n$

$n$ is a variable.

**Venn diagram** A diagram that uses circles to show the relationship among sets of objects.

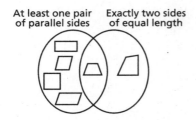

At least one pair of parallel sides    Exactly two sides of equal length

**vertex** A point where sides, rays, or edges meet.

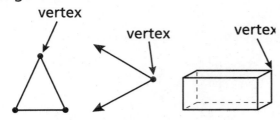

vertex    vertex    vertex

**vertical** Extending in two directions, up and down.

**vertical bar graph** A bar graph with vertical bars.

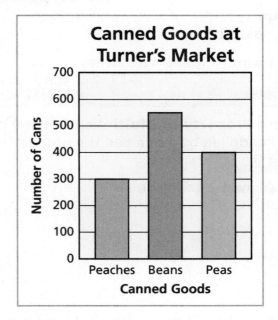

## W

**weight** The measure of how heavy something is.

**word form** A name of a number written using words instead of digits.

**Example:** Nine hundred eighty-four

# Glossary (continued)

## Y

**yard (yd)** A customary unit used to measure length.

1 yard = 3 feet = 36 inches

## Z

**Zero Property of Multiplication** If 0 is multiplied by a number, the product is 0.

Example: $3 \times 0 = 0$

# Multiplication Table and Scrambled Tables (Volume 1)

## A

| × | 1 | 2 | 3 | 4 | 5 | 6 | 7 | 8 | 9 | 10 |
|---|---|---|---|---|---|---|---|---|---|----|
| 1 | 1 | 2 | 3 | 4 | 5 | 6 | 7 | 8 | 9 | 10 |
| 2 | 2 | 4 | 6 | 8 | 10 | 12 | 14 | 16 | 18 | 20 |
| 3 | 3 | 6 | 9 | 12 | 15 | 18 | 21 | 24 | 27 | 30 |
| 4 | 4 | 8 | 12 | 16 | 20 | 24 | 28 | 32 | 36 | 40 |
| 5 | 5 | 10 | 15 | 20 | 25 | 30 | 35 | 40 | 45 | 50 |
| 6 | 6 | 12 | 18 | 24 | 30 | 36 | 42 | 48 | 54 | 60 |
| 7 | 7 | 14 | 21 | 28 | 35 | 42 | 49 | 56 | 63 | 70 |
| 8 | 8 | 16 | 24 | 32 | 40 | 48 | 56 | 64 | 72 | 80 |
| 9 | 9 | 18 | 27 | 36 | 45 | 54 | 63 | 72 | 81 | 90 |
| 10 | 10 | 20 | 30 | 40 | 50 | 60 | 70 | 80 | 90 | 100 |

## B

| × | 2 | 4 | 3 | 1 | 5 | 10 | 6 | 8 | 7 | 9 |
|---|---|---|---|---|---|----|---|---|---|---|
| 5 | 10 | 20 | 15 | 5 | 25 | 50 | 30 | 40 | 35 | 45 |
| 3 | 6 | 12 | 9 | 3 | 15 | 30 | 18 | 24 | 21 | 27 |
| 1 | 2 | 4 | 3 | 1 | 5 | 10 | 6 | 8 | 7 | 9 |
| 4 | 8 | 16 | 12 | 4 | 20 | 40 | 24 | 32 | 28 | 36 |
| 2 | 4 | 8 | 6 | 2 | 10 | 20 | 12 | 16 | 14 | 18 |
| 7 | 14 | 28 | 21 | 7 | 35 | 70 | 42 | 56 | 49 | 63 |
| 9 | 18 | 36 | 27 | 9 | 45 | 90 | 54 | 72 | 63 | 81 |
| 10 | 20 | 40 | 30 | 10 | 50 | 100 | 60 | 80 | 70 | 90 |
| 8 | 16 | 32 | 24 | 8 | 40 | 80 | 48 | 64 | 56 | 72 |
| 6 | 12 | 24 | 18 | 6 | 30 | 60 | 36 | 48 | 42 | 54 |

## C

| × | 8 | 6 | 4 | 9 | 7 | 9 | 6 | 7 | 4 | 8 |
|---|---|---|---|---|---|---|---|---|---|---|
| 5 | 40 | 30 | 20 | 45 | 35 | 45 | 30 | 35 | 20 | 40 |
| 3 | 24 | 18 | 12 | 27 | 21 | 27 | 18 | 21 | 12 | 24 |
| 2 | 16 | 12 | 8 | 18 | 14 | 18 | 12 | 14 | 8 | 16 |
| 3 | 24 | 18 | 12 | 27 | 21 | 27 | 18 | 21 | 12 | 24 |
| 5 | 40 | 30 | 20 | 45 | 35 | 45 | 30 | 35 | 20 | 40 |
| 9 | 72 | 54 | 36 | 81 | 63 | 81 | 54 | 63 | 36 | 72 |
| 4 | 32 | 24 | 16 | 36 | 28 | 36 | 24 | 28 | 16 | 32 |
| 7 | 56 | 42 | 28 | 63 | 49 | 63 | 42 | 49 | 28 | 56 |
| 6 | 48 | 36 | 24 | 54 | 42 | 54 | 36 | 42 | 24 | 48 |
| 8 | 64 | 48 | 32 | 72 | 56 | 72 | 48 | 56 | 32 | 64 |

## D

| × | 6 | 7 | 8 | 7 | 8 | 6 | 7 | 8 | 6 | 8 |
|---|---|---|---|---|---|---|---|---|---|---|
| 2 | 12 | 14 | 16 | 14 | 16 | 12 | 14 | 16 | 12 | 16 |
| 3 | 18 | 21 | 24 | 21 | 24 | 18 | 21 | 24 | 18 | 24 |
| 4 | 24 | 28 | 32 | 28 | 32 | 24 | 28 | 32 | 24 | 32 |
| 5 | 30 | 35 | 40 | 35 | 40 | 30 | 35 | 40 | 30 | 40 |
| 7 | 42 | 49 | 56 | 49 | 56 | 42 | 49 | 56 | 42 | 56 |
| 8 | 48 | 56 | 64 | 56 | 64 | 48 | 56 | 64 | 48 | 64 |
| 6 | 36 | 42 | 48 | 42 | 48 | 36 | 42 | 48 | 36 | 48 |
| 9 | 54 | 63 | 72 | 63 | 72 | 54 | 63 | 72 | 54 | 72 |
| 8 | 48 | 56 | 64 | 56 | 64 | 48 | 56 | 64 | 48 | 64 |
| 6 | 36 | 42 | 48 | 42 | 48 | 36 | 42 | 48 | 36 | 48 |